INTERNATIONAL SOCIALISM

A quarterly journal of socialist theory

Winter 1993

Contents

Issue 61 of INTERNATIONAL SOCIALISM, quarterly journal of the Socialist Workers Party (Britain)

Published December 1993
Copyright © International Socialism
Distribution/subscriptions: International Socialism,
PO Box 82, London E3.
American distribution: B de Boer, 113 East Center St, Nutley,
New Jersey 07110.
Subscriptions and back copies: PO Box 16085, Chicago
Illinois 60616
Editorial and production: 071-538 1626/071-538 0538
Sales and subscriptions: 071-538 5821
American sales: 312 666 7337

ISBN 0905-998839

Printed by BPCC Wheatons Ltd, Exeter, England
Typeset by East End Offset, London E3

Cover design by Tim Sanders

For details of back copies see the end pages of this book

Subscription rates for one year (four issues) are:

Britain and overseas (surface):	individual	£12.00 ($25)
	institutional	£20.00
Air speeded supplement:	North America	nil
	Europe/South America	£1.00
	elsewhere	£2.00

Note to contributors
The deadline for articles intended for issue 62 of
International Socialism is 1 February 1994

All contributions should be double-spaced with wide margins.
Please submit two copies. If you write your contribution
using a computer, please also supply a disk, together with
details of the computer and programme used.

INTERNATIONAL SOCIALISM ★

A quarterly journal of socialist theory

JOHN MAJOR was supposed to be the Tories' saviour after Thatcherism. Now his premiership looks as weak as Thatcher's ever did. But behind the splits in the Tory party lies the much greater crisis of British society. Lindsey German first analysed that crisis in 'The last days of Thatcher', published in *International Socialism 48* just as Thatcher's regime fell to pieces. Here she updates her examination of Tory Britain, charting its economic weakness, its social decay, the strengths and weaknesses of the Labour Party and the trade union movement and the prospects for socialists.

'POLITICAL CORRECTNESS' was a scare started by the right in academia and the press. But it involves issues which no socialist can duck. John Molyneux plots a careful course through the arguments. He damns the hypocrisy of the right but shows that socialists should not be uncritical supporters of much of what is done in the name of political correctness.

E P THOMPSON was a powerful advocate of Marxism's central role in explaining historical change. He was also an unrepentant enemy of academic phrase-mongering and a lifelong political activist. Dave McNally's obituary highlights Thompson's considerable strengths and suggests how his legacy can best be extended.

JAZZ MUSIC comes under Charlie Hore's critical eye and the Labour Party's decline is examined by Charlie Kimber in the latest *Bookwatch*.

Editor: John Rees, Assistant Editors: Alex Callinicos, Sue Clegg, Chris Harman, John Molyneux, Lindsey German, Ann Rogers, Colin Sparks, Mike Gonzalez, Peter Morgan, Ruth Brown, Mike Haynes and Rob Hoveman.

Before the flood?

LINDSEY GERMAN

Riots, slump, decay and despair: these are the results of John Major's term in office. The Tory party which briefly united around Major just three years ago, and rejoiced at his re-election 18 months later, is now deeply divided on every issue from Europe to taxation, from Bosnia to privatisation. Its divisions reflect a much wider ideological splintering as the different ruling class interests which grouped together in the 1980s under the hegemony of Thatcherism find themselves bitterly divided.

Economic collapse has undermined the ideological certainty. Perhaps the most intense opposition to the Tories stems from many who once accepted Tory policies. Now they feel betrayed. This leaves even the ruling class with no real confidence that the present government can do anything to end the economic and social crisis which has them in its grip. This is a huge change in the political climate.

Thatcher was able to impose her policies not because she never compromised—the ludicrous claim made in her memoirs—but because the ruling class in Britain largely accepted the Thatcherite project in the 1980s. There was widespread opposition to the early government policies during the recession of 1980-81, especially from manufacturing industry. But once the economy began to grow again, that resistance began to disappear. By 1986 and 1987, when powerful groups of workers had already been defeated, when the economy was growing very fast and when even unemployment figures were falling, Britain's rulers really did begin to believe that the Thatcher miracle had worked, that slump was a thing of the past and that Britain could lead Europe economically and politically.

The reversal of economic fortunes exposed the solution of the 1980s as a sham. The British ruling class was faced with uncomfortable choices. The argument over entry into the Exchange Rate Mechanism of the European Monetary System was about these choices. The options were to become a junior partner in the EC on relatively unfavourable terms, or stay outside a fully integrated Europe on even more unfavourable terms. The political crisis which erupted on Black Wednesday, 15 September 1992, when the pound was forced out of the ERM, laid bare these splits. The prestige of the Tory government has never recovered. As Tory right winger Simon Heffer put it recently, 'The worst problem facing the Tory Party...is that the government has still not rebuilt its moral authority after the political catastrophe of Black Wednesday 13 months ago.'[1]

The crisis at the top is partly a reflection of and partly creates a crisis among the lower middle classes. The popular dissatisfaction and bitterness among the traditionally stable backbone of the Conservative Party is now rampant. It is all the more fierce for coming from people who placed absolute faith in Thatcherism but who now find their businesses bankrupted, their homes repossessed and even managerial jobs under attack. The political alliance which included the ruling class, most of the middle classes and substantial sections of workers has broken down. It was symbolised by Rupert Murdoch's *Sun*, whose uncritical and enthusiastic reflection of Thatcherism conveyed many of its ideas in popular form. Any cursory glance at the paper in the days following Black Wednesday reveals how that enthusiasm has been turned to angry opposition, reflecting a sense of betrayal.

Among many workers too there has been a sharp political shift. The effect of the market has produced a political revulsion among many people who were once tempted to believe in its miraculous qualities. At the root of this change in political mood has been the attack on workers' living standards through the poll tax and the accelerated assault on the welfare state. Millions of workers who thought themselves secure have found themselves disillusioned. Since the election Major's premiership has been exposed as weak, indecisive, unpleasant and vindictive, and quite often unable to carry a majority of people with it in any of its central policies. Far from the Major years representing a period of calm following the turbulence of Thatcherism, they have produced a level of discontent and anger, and increased politicisation, greater than anything seen in Britain for many years.

Recession and stagnation have marked Major's entire period of office. Options supposedly available to buy the Tories out of their problems, for example the 'windfall' subsidy provided by North Sea oil in the early to mid-1980s, or the injections of billions of pounds' worth of public money to win the miners' strike of 1984-5 are simply no longer available. At an individual level workers have found that their jobs are no longer secure as unemployment has soared, wages have been held down and overtime has disappeared.

The effect of the Tories' crisis has been that their 'mandate' won in the 1992 election has effectively been eroded. The rot began just three months after the election victory. CBI boss Howard Davies was calling for a wage freeze, there was a sterling crisis and the stench of corruption, scandal and decay around the government even before the crises over the ERM and pit closures.

Tory and ruling class hopes that signs of economic recovery would restore their fortunes have so far proved false. The internal crisis of the Tory party as well as its disastrous showing in opinion polls by the spring and summer of 1993 (between 23 and 28 percent in August 1993) indicate that the Tories are as unpopular as ever.[2]

And yet among socialists and trade unionists there is still a great deal of unease. Labour is well ahead in the opinion polls (but it has been before) and its leadership seems incapable of giving either voice or direction to protests. The feeling of October 1992, when hundreds of thousands marched for the miners and succeeded in shaking the government to its foundations, has been allowed to dissipate. Subsequent strikes at the Timex factory in Dundee and at University College Hospital in London succeeded in galvanising very wide layers of support but did not mark signal victories.

The significant numbers of one day or half day strikes which take place tend to remain under the control of the trade union leaders. Meanwhile, job losses seem to pile up without any action against them, conditions in virtually every workplace are under attack—in both the private and the public sectors—and wage increases are at very low levels. Union membership still seems to be falling inexorably, the number of strike days is extremely low and the unions are repeatedly described as 'dinosaurs' by government and media alike.

So is it all an illusion? Will the discontent and anger find an outlet in mass strikes which can defeat the government and reverse the years of attacks on workers which were such a feature of the 1980s, or will it be dispersed by lack of clear direction and leadership? Even worse, with last year's victory of the BNP candidate in the Isle of Dogs, will the mood of bitterness turn in a much nastier direction, with racism being used to divide and rule those workers who have suffered so much from the crisis?

Will the Tories and the ruling class manage to regain the offensive, scoring a significant defeat against workers' organisation? Or will the working class movement eventually succeed in rolling back some of these attacks? The sort of stand off between the two sides which we have witnessed over the past three years cannot, after all, continue indefinitely. What are the prospects?

Great expectations?

The most frequently expressed hope of Tory politicians is that everything will come right when the economy does. Then, it is said, their popularity will return. The disaffection of millions of erstwhile Tory supporters will disappear, according to this view, if they can once again afford to buy houses and consumer durables, go on holidays and earn higher real wages. That means returning security to the jobs market and ensuring that earnings rise. This in turn means replacing the recession and stagnation of the past three years with a new boom. Recovery will both create a mood of contentment among those now disaffected with the government, and obviate unpopular or difficult governmental decisions. Increasing taxation, for example, will be unnecessary if economic growth is sufficient. Right wing cabinet minister John Redwood described this scenario in a recent interview:

> *I think we are now coming out of recession quite quickly. I think commentators are estimating the extent of the recovery already. That is becoming manifest in new car sales, developments in the housing market and it is certainly fully recognised by the stock market which has been hitting new highs for many months. There has been a rush by private investors to participate now that the market has risen quite a long way. I think all that is really quite positive. Looking to the future, I see a good period for strengthening and broadening the base of popular capitalism.*[3]

On this analysis, the most superficial aspects of recovery will be sufficient to win new devotees of 'popular capitalism', ready once again to buy their council houses and stocks and shares, to set up their small businesses and to buy their new company cars. It is the Tory ideal, and as remote from reality as most idealised pictures. Nonetheless, a parallel view is also promoted by sections of the left, including much of the Labour leadership. They do not believe in 'popular capitalism', but believe that most workers do. Any dissatisfaction with the government is shortlived, they argue, and will disappear when there is money in workers' pockets.

But Tory optimists and Labour cynics are wrong on both counts: the Thatcher-Lawson boom cannot be repeated in the near future, and any economic upturn is unlikely to eradicate the sorts of difficulties which the Tories face. The government cannot look forward to an easy solution to their economic problems—and so will not be able to solve their political problems.

Hopes of economic recovery are absolutely central to the Tories' political strategy. Such a recovery is, according to various government sources, just around the corner. Just as they found the recession shocking precisely because it was so inexplicable, so they expect recovery to be like blue skies after rain. They are likely to be sorely disillusioned. There is no certainty of sustained recovery. It is true that expectations are high, with the majority of surveys of bosses and managers revealing an optimistic future for sustained growth of their industries. But expectations are not matched by hard facts. One typical survey—among manufacturing employers—showed a high degree of optimism, with 57 percent of companies predicting growth of up to 10 percent during 1993, while another 26 percent saw growth at over 10 percent this year. A staggering 96 percent believed their companies would grow significantly over the next three years. But, as the author of the survey pointed out:

> Given their failure to meet 1992's targets, however, it seems that Britain's manufacturers are being over optimistic. How will they achieve such a major reversal in their fortunes? Is an economic upturn of the magnitude necessary to support this predicted growth really 'just around the corner'?[4]

The optimism is certainly not matched by the facts. There was growth in Gross Domestic Product during the first half of 1993, but it remained very slight, with output still well below the figure when recession began. Recovery has also been patchy and uneven, with some sectors of the economy doing much better than others. There is no hard evidence that this recovery can be sustained. Even government figures have had to be revised downwards. Earlier in 1993 it was estimated that manufacturing output since autumn 1992 had grown by more than 3 percent—that figure has had to be cut nearly in half to 1.8 percent.[5] Other figures registered a larger than expected fall in manufacturing investment in the second quarter of 1993 after several quarters of slow upward growth.[6] A recent CBI survey showed that manufacturing order books had fallen from earlier 1993 levels in the majority of its regions.[7] Treasury statistics issued in the autumn of 1993 pointed to a slight slowdown in growth which was at only 0.4 percent (excluding oil and gas) between July and September. But manufacturing output actually shrank, and one economist cautioned that the figures were anyway 'extremely unreliable', while another said that 'the economy is starting to slow down'.[8]

Reports of a sustained recovery are therefore much exaggerated, and there is every possibility that the pattern of recovery will at best be similar to the United States in the past year: low levels of growth which peter out, then re-emerge, but never really develop. Very few jobs are created and many problems of the recession, such as huge levels of debt, remain central features.

Recession affected Britain much earlier and much more deeply than virtually any of its major competitors. 'Recovery to what?' is therefore a real question in an economy where 'UK output fell by 4 percent between the second quarter of 1990 and the second quarter of 1992 and has not yet returned to its level at the beginning of 1989'.[9] The August 1993 poll of economic forecasters in the *Economist* projected UK growth at 1.6 percent and at 2.6 percent for 1994. This is a better rate than most of its European competitors who have only recently gone into recession, but compares highly unfavourably with projections for the US, Canada and Australia (the other long standing victims of 'Anglo-Saxon recession').[10] The current boast of government ministers, that Britain's will be the fastest growing economy in Europe in 1993, is misleading. The big European economies were growing quite strongly during the early 1990s when output in Britain was falling.[11] In any case, Britain's export markets are heavily connected to countries such as Germany. Recession there affects British capitalism, as the recent layoffs at the big car factories have shown. Despite an upturn in car sales in Britain, the car market in continental Europe shrank dramatically during 1993, thus affecting exports from Britain.[12]

Is British capitalism therefore in a position to compete with its main rivals and so solve its problems even if a recovery is sustained? The answer is no, if past performance, even during the booming 1980s, is a guide. If we date growth back to 1979, rather than to the end of recession in 1981 as the Tories prefer to do, we find that the total increase in output in manufacturing industry during that period was 7 percent. Manufacturing capacity increased by the same amount—not bad for Europe, but lagging behind the US and Japan where capacity grew by 32 percent and 39 percent respectively. If we go further back, British manufacturing capacity between 1970 and 1990 grew by 19 percent, but by 43 percent in the big three European economies, 86 percent in the US and 129 percent in Japan.[13] Although there has been an increase in investment in manufacturing capacity, this may not reflect a growth in jobs or output but rather that 'the UK may simply be replacing the wrong sort of capacity with more efficient and up-to-date equipment'. If this is the case, 'the danger is that Britain will still be left with a small and efficient manufacturing sector that is too small for the nation's future prosperity'.[14]

Inability to compete through lack of a sufficiently large manufacturing sector can be compounded by the other problems facing British capitalism, some of them products of the recession, others the legacy of the Lawson boom: high unemployment, bankruptcies, a colossal debt hangover, lack of investment, a record public sector borrowing deficit and a balance of trade deficit which threatens to suck in even more imports when economic upturn comes. Budget deficit and public debt—far from being eradicated, as we were told in the late 1980s—are likely to remain a running sore in the British economy for a long time to come. Recent projections by the International Monetary Fund about the budget deficits show just how serious this problem is:

> *The UK in particular is on an explosive course: by 1998, its budget deficit is expected to remain more than twice as great as that needed to stabilise its debt ratio. Little wonder that the IMF privately fears that the debt threat is moving north. These days it is the build-up of first world debt, not Africa's lingering crisis, that haunts the sleep of IMF officials.*[15]

Unemployment levels remain high despite minute falls in the jobless levels through the summer of 1993—with official figures of 3 million and an overall rate of 10.4 percent.[16] The jobs which we were told had been created by the Lawson boom of the mid-1980s have simply not been sustained. The figures are fairly staggering. Employment fell by 1.4 million between 1979 and 1983 during the first Thatcher recession. It then rose during the boom to not only replace those lost but create another 1.9 million jobs in total. However, since 1990 the second Thatcher recession has removed nearly all of these jobs—with only half a million net extra jobs being created since 1978! 'Over the period 1979-92, US employment grew by 19 percent, French employment by 3 percent and UK employment by 0.4 percent.'[17]

So expansion of employment—even in the low wage, low tech jobs which have marked much of the new employment in recent years—has been negligible. But perhaps the greatest hidden fear of the employers is that an increase in industrial output and signs of real recovery will lead to demands for big wage increases. Wage rises have been held down in recent years through a combination of low inflation, recession and lack of industrial struggle. The Tory government has insisted on a wage freeze in the public sector for 1994. Its aim is to put down a marker to private industry (it fears that private sector wage increases will get out of control) while at the same time taking a hard line on public spending.[18] But the political backlash against the government is in large part a result of its assault on public sector spending so far. Attacks on a wider front are only likely to raise the level of general political opposition to the Tories' policies and to ruling class strategy. It is to this that we now turn.

Breaking all the records

> *At the very least, if we are to live within a market capitalist system, it is unsatisfactory that we should have doubts about its moral foundations. One or two*

recent speeches, even by some members of the present government, betray a worrying insecurity... Once the legitimacy of egalitarianism is accepted, however much equality there is, the cry will always be for more of it.[19]

These were the words of Lord Lawson of Blaby who in his previous incarnation as Chancellor of the Exchequer presided over the frothy boom of the late 1980s, the overheating of the economy and the onset of slump. His is the authentic voice of 1980s Thatcherism: confident, arrogant and a passionate advocate of inequality. Like Gordon Gekko in the film *Wall Street*, Lawson believes that 'greed is good'. Such views could be echoed by half a dozen former cabinet ministers who also now sit in the House of Lords.

Yet despite the excesses of the 1993 Tory party conference with its attempts to find scapegoats among single parents, 'foreigners' and young criminals, there are still not many of the present cabinet who would dare to be so blatant as Lawson. Most pretend that they are more committed to egalitarianism, to choice, against the excesses of the very wealthy. Yet very few people believe them. They are, if anything, even more unpopular than their predecessors. As a recent *Daily Telegraph* article pointed out, 'the government and the Conservative Party continue to establish new records in Gallup's surveys'. These new records include that 'the proportion of voters "approving" of the government's record, 12.2 percent, has remained below 20 percent for 10 months...a tiny 23 percent of voters now say they would back the Conservatives...fewer than 20 percent of voters are "satisfied" with Mr Major as prime minister... No previous prime minister ever fell below 20 percent.'[20]

Why are they so unpopular? After all, when Major replaced Thatcher in the winter of 1990 he had offended few people even inside the Tory party, let alone outside. He had the virtue of not being Margaret Thatcher, which alone raised his popularity a few notches, and he fought the leadership campaign largely on the claim that he understood ordinary people because he had spent a short period of his life in Brixton. Today he is pilloried in the newspapers, hated by many in his own party and despised by millions of working people.

There are three main components of this dramatic change in fortune: the Tories' own political mistakes, the worsening and intractable problems which face the mass of ordinary workers, and the increased politicisation of millions of people.

The Tories' own mistakes

It was commonplace for both the Major cabinet and the press to assume that the removal of Thatcher would restore Tory popularity. Consequently there was little if any attempt to alter most of the policies which had contributed to her growing unpopularity. This was even true of the poll tax, where Major and Heseltine were reluctant to completely abandon the notion of a tax on individuals, and where the final form of the council tax was a hybrid between a property and a personal tax.[21] Levels of non-payment remained extremely high. Months after Thatcher's departure thousands were still being taken to court for refusing to pay. Although the levels of poll tax were held down in March 1991 by adding 2.5 percent to the level of value added tax, the poll tax itself was only finally abolished in March of 1993.

John Major had the briefest 'honeymoon', which did not even last through the Gulf War, preventing him from exploiting that victory in the way that Thatcher had done with the Falklands War in 1982. The simple explanation for his failure was the terrible impact of the recession, whose adverse affects seemed to be accelerating daily by the spring of 1991 when the figures for unemployment hit 2 million.[22] Everyone could see it coming. Two thousand five hundred workers were sacked in a single day in January 1992 from firms including Peugeot, Ford, BICC and NatWest. British Airways announced 4,600 jobs to go, and British Steel 800.[23] By February 1,500 were losing their jobs every day.

The government was completely paralysed by the recession and its political consequences. It had no clear idea what to do, veering from complete inactivity to Norman Lamont's declaration that unemployment was 'a price worth paying' to get inflation down. If it was tempted to buy its way out of problems, this was not apparent. The recession meant pressure to keep spending low. The ideological commitment to Thatcherism and a remoteness from the concerns of ordinary people all compounded its unpopularity.

During the heyday of Thatcher's rule the Ridley Plan—to isolate and then defeat different groups of workers—successfully guided government strategy. Major's government, in contrast, acted in ways which only worsened its position by uniting those opposed to it. The government continued and sometimes accelerated its attacks on welfare, the health service, housing and jobs. It pushed through vicious attacks if it thought it could get away with them, but its weakness meant that it could also easily be forced to retreat if it met even limited opposition.

So in late 1991 and early 1992 it increased levels of public spending and retreated from or avoided a whole number of potential industrial confrontations. The rail workers, for example, found British Rail's 'final offer' of 7 percent was upped to nearly 8 percent.[24] Money was found to bring down the NHS waiting lists in the months before the election. The promises were that recovery was just around the corner—and growth would mean taxes could stay low, spending would not have to be cut, new jobs would be created.

But two events soon pushed government standing to new lows. Black Wednesday, 15 September 1992, was the day Major and Lamont spent billions of pounds shoring up the pound to no avail, and demonstrated their willingness to raise interest rates by 5 percent in a matter of hours. There could not have been a greater blow to a government which claimed there was no more money for hospitals or schools, and which said it had the interests of mortgage holders at heart. And Black Wednesday contributed to the mood of anger and hostility which erupted just a month later on the announcement that 31 pits were to be closed, effectively destroying the coal industry and the lives of whole communities.

Since then Major's unpopularity has been constant, as he stumbles from crisis to crisis over the Maastricht Treaty (only ratified through a deal with the Ulster Unionists and arm twisting of Tory rebels), the universally unpopular VAT on fuel and the retreat on testing in schools and other Tory education 'reforms'. Various leaks of proposed cuts in social security spending such as raising the pension age of both sexes to 67 or of women to 65, cutting invalidity benefit or restricting unemployment benefit to six months instead of a year, have all contributed to this unpopularity.

The once reliable loyalty of Tory supporters is no longer certain, as the Tories' catastrophic defeats in the Newbury and Christchurch by-elections show. Even members of the Tory party, including loyal activists, are extremely disaffected, though this manifests itself in the paradox both of nostalgia for the 'strong government' of Thatcher and disquiet at the attacks on welfare. Two long standing party activists, a retired surgeon and a dentist in Cheshire, were quoted in a recent *Observer* magazine feature:

> *I think the way* [Thatcher] *was got rid of was appalling. I honestly remember thinking I didn't want to have anything more to do with the party. We all reluctantly felt after she had gone we should have Major. I think we all thought he was a very nice man. Then he came in and won the election and it has all gone from bad to worse.*

They cite their main objections to the government as the defence of David Mellor by John Major, Major's failure to call a referendum on the Maastricht Treaty, the Matrix-Churchill case and 'the most appalling thing was the miners: we just looked like a party that didn't care at all. Totally insensitive. And that got people really upset. I don't think they showed any compassion or respect'.[25]

Similar attitudes were shown when John Major visited the West Country after losing the Christchurch by-election. The local Tory membership officer said, 'It's a very loyal party but it's had the worst year ever.'[26] The 1993 Conservative Party conference in Blackpool contained fewer local representatives—'there were fewer of them this year, many regulars having suffered such a crash of morale that they did not attend.'[27]

The demoralisation among those who a few years ago would have been the enthusiastic cheerleaders of Margaret Thatcher gives some notion of the ideological collapse of 'popular Toryism' and indeed 'popular capitalism'. The collapse seems provoked by two aspects of the crisis: from the ravages of the system itself as boom has turned into slump and forced unemployment and poverty on millions who once believed they could find a comfortable niche within the system and, at the top of the social pile, the behaviour of the Tory government, big businessmen and others close to it, who have been revealed as greedy, corrupt, sleazy and unprincipled. Public outcry over top directors' pay or over business funding of the Tory party is an indicator of this.

But these factors alone clearly cannot explain the political shift which has taken place since Thatcher went. During the 1980s there were equally huge increases in top people's pay, funding of the Tories by big business was equally prevalent and there was as much corruption. Nor can the change be explained by John Major's personality—he became leader of the Tories precisely because he did not have the force of personality of Thatcher. The real reason lies with much more fundamental problems which it will take much more than cosmetic changes to alter.

Put simply, the economic difficulties facing British capitalism are much more severe than problems created by a single recession. Britain's declining standing as a great power internationally has left it with a legacy of spending, particularly in the areas of defence and welfare, which are no longer sustainable without taking much more from workers in the form of taxation, or else cutting into profits. But the government has so far been unable or unwilling to do either, and so has had to continue funding public spending at an even higher level than in the late 1980s.[28] The boom hid, but did not solve, this problem which has come back to haunt the Tories with a vengeance.

The worsening situation for most workers

'A nation at ease with itself' is hardly how most people would describe life in Britain today. Here is the view of financial journalist Christopher Huhne:

> *In time, our form of capitalism will come to resemble the American variety. We will not regard ourselves as part of a society, but merely as individuals who must fend for ourselves as best we may, and devil take the hindmost.*
>
> *With even more of the poor always with us, we will not seek to provide security as a public good; we will buy burglar and car alarms, anti-theft*

*radios, private picket gates. We will earn more and spend more just to main-
tain the same sense of security we had when society was kinder and fairer. We
will drive from a night-watchman-protected dormitory through ghettoes of the
underclass to security-coded office buildings. Shut out the world, we want to
be rich—whatever the cost.*[29]

While this picture depicts the 'yuppie nightmare' which many
national newspaper journalists no doubt fear, it also portrays a popular
view of 1990s Britain—even if from the other side of the fence to most
of us. Society is more violent, the 'old values' have broken down, there
is a growing gap between rich and poor, and any idea of consensus politics has completely disappeared.

Certainly those who believed that the old evils of capitalism were
gradually disappearing to be replaced with a more just, fairer society have
been sorely disappointed. The Beveridge Report published in 1942 indi-
cated the great problems of British society which needed to be
eradicated—want, ignorance, disease, squalor and idleness. The basis of
the post-war welfare state, and the political ideas which underpinned it,
were intended to ensure that these miseries disappeared. Full employment, a national health service, council house building and adequate state
benefits for the old, sick and disabled were regarded as its foundations.

The reality has turned out rather different. Unemployment is running
at 10 percent of the population overall, the male rate being even higher.[30]
The real situation is much worse than the figures indicate. Many men
who would previously have been classified as unemployed are now cat-
egorised as 'economically inactive'. 'On average in the 1980s…14.9
percent of UK prime age males were out of work.'[31] Poverty has grown,
with 11.33 million people on or below the supplementary benefit/income
support level in 1989 compared with 7.74 in 1979.[32] The decline of NHS
funding has meant an alarming rise in preventible diseases such as
dysentery. NHS provision is inadequate in many areas. For example,
14,000 babies in need of special care were, according to one report, competing for only 800 beds, two thirds of which were paid for by charities.[33]
In 1992, 400,000 people were registered as homeless, but the housing
charity Shelter puts the real figure at closer to 2 million. Around 150,000
young people become homeless each year.[34] Those with houses are not
always so much better off. Although in the last two decades there has
been a sharp reduction in the number of houses lacking amenities (such
as baths, inside toilets, hot and cold running water), there has been only
a marginal reduction in the number of 'unfit' dwellings, and an actual
increase in the number of those in serious disrepair.[35]

The sense of decay pervading Britain comes from the worsening situation in all these areas. The slashing of capital spending on hospitals,
schools, housing and other areas of infrastructure has resulted in virtu-

ally every publicly funded building being in need of repair, redecoration or complete rebuilding. The contrast between the public and private sectors could not be greater.

However, we should not assume that this picture of decay is one which only affects an 'underclass.' The attacks on welfare, jobs, housing and health care affect the vast majority of the population. We should be wary of assuming that figures for inequality of income distribution apply only to the very rich and the very poor. There is no doubt that the gap between rich and poor has widened, but the full picture of British society is not at all what the ruling class and the middle class commentators would have us believe.

Poverty is supposedly restricted to a small minority of those living mainly on state benefits. So Christopher Huhne quotes a recent government report arguing that it demonstrates that the bottom 10 percent in Britain 'have suffered real falls in their income since 1979 despite the enormous increases for everyone else'.[36]

But 'everyone else' has not done quite as well as Huhne and others imply. They have certainly not been the recipients of 'enormous increases'. Basing its figures on the government's own statistics, the Commission on Social Justice has demonstrated that nearly two thirds of the population have an income below the average.[37] This hardly fits in with the 'two thirds prosperous, one third poor' image we are constantly bombarded with by, among others, Labour leader John Smith. Indeed, the past 15 years have shown a marked move away from egalitarianism towards a widening gap between rich and poor—not just the poorest. So 'the bottom half of the population now receive only a quarter of the total income, compared to a third in 1979'.[38] In addition, changes in income for the bottom half of the population are demonstrative. It is true that average income rose 36 percent per household between 1979 and 1990-91.[39] But the share of the bottom tenth declined by 14 percent, that of the second bottom tenth stayed the same, the third, fourth and fifth lowest share increased by 7, 16 and 22 percent respectively—all much less than the average.

A small proportion of the rich have got much richer. Even government figures which tend to underestimate real ownership of wealth show that the top 2 percent own a quarter of all wealth, and the top 10 percent a full half of all wealth.[40] And 'of the £31 billion given away in tax cuts between 1979 and 1992, 27 percent or £8.7 billion went to the top 1 percent of income earners. £15.2 billion went to the top 10 percent and 15 percent or £4.8 billion went to the bottom 50 percent.'[41]

The net result of this redistribution in favour of the rich has been to leave the mass of those *in work* far from comfortably off. A chart produced by the Commission on Social Justice recently demonstrated that 36.7 million people live on incomes below £250 per week. Only half a million earn over £1,000 a week.[42] The average weekly disposable income for households stands at £280.04, with average family expenditure at £272.10. But expenditure is rising at twice the level of inflation.[43] The bulk of that income is spent on essentials. A whacking £95.70 is spent on or around the house, if the costs of housing, fuel, light and power, and household goods and services are taken together. Another £47.70 goes on food and £42.90 on motoring and travel, leaving £85.80 per week for every other bit of family expenditure: clothes, holidays, books and newspapers, sports and entertainment, alcohol and tobacco.[44]

Many of the families eligible for the family credit benefit do not claim it because they do not realise they are meant to be 'poor'. Explaining the failure of this benefit to reach more than 64 percent of eligible families, a recent survey concluded that 'they did not realise they were entitled to means tested benefit. They tended to be white collar couples who were buying their own home.'[45]

What's happening to pay?

During the 1980s wages rose in real terms for most workers (although benefits for pensioners and those on social security, as well as student grants, failed to keep pace). Attacks on welfare, anti-union laws and privatisation were accompanied by significant wage rises in many areas, which helped to prevent more general industrial opposition to government policies. Most people therefore felt themselves better off year by year. As Hugo Young has put it, writing of the 1987 election campaign:

> *Inflation did not rise above 5 percent at any point during this parliament. In the four years after the 1983 election, average weekly earnings rose by 14 percent in real terms... All employed people, therefore, felt better off, even if ministers had made a mess of the rest of their programme.*[46]

This remained the case up to the 1992 election, since fear of confrontation over pay led to substantial increases in a whole number of industries.

Now there are signs that the situation is beginning to change. Government figures recently revealed that 'pre-tax personal incomes between April and June [1993] showed their first quarterly fall for 27 years, partly because of low wage increases, a fall in social security benefits and weaker investment income.'[47]

Indeed, it would appear that manual workers have seen their living standards and wage levels held below the rate of inflation, while managerial and administrative white collar grades have been rewarded with increases much higher than the average. If we add to this the effects of short time working, lay offs, periods of unemployment and a cutback in overtime, we can see that the financial situation of many workers, especially manual workers, has deteriorated fairly sharply in the last year or two. The lower paid, who include the bulk of manual workers, have been disproportionately hard hit.

The government's latest *New Earnings Survey* shows that manual workers have been particularly badly hit, with average manual wages only increasing by 2.5 percent, compared with a rise of 4.4 percent for non-manual occupations. These averages hide the extent to which managers' pay has risen much faster than routine white collar workers. Some workers suffered real wage cuts in 1992-93. Non-manual women workers under 18 suffered pay cuts of 9.3 percent, and all full time women workers under 18 saw pay cuts of 5.9 percent. Royal Mail manual workers, for example, also suffered a pay cut of 3.2 percent.

The survey gave the weekly average male manual gross wage at £274.30, while non-manuals averaged £418.20. Women manuals averaged £177.10 and non-manuals £268.70. Despite the claims of Labour's leadership several years ago that dockers were earning £400 a week, even at 1993 levels, 89.1 percent of male manual workers had gross weekly earnings of less than that amount.[48]

These figures are the result of squeezes on both the private and public sector wage levels. A Confederation of British Industry survey put manufacturing industry pay rises between April and June 1993 at 2.3 percent, the lowest for at least 16 years. It also claimed that 'pay freezes of less than 12 months are widespread, affecting about one in three manufacturers and one in four service sector companies'.[49] There are disputes about whether private sector pay settlements are now beginning to rise again. For example, Incomes Data Services argues that the number of pay deals between 2 and 4 percent is rising, and the number of pay freezes and pay pauses is declining.[50] There is no doubt, however, that the level of wage increases has remained low and shows little sign of dramatic change.

The current public sector pay freeze is at least partly justified by the Tories on the grounds that public sector pay is rising at faster levels than private sector. But, while it is true that for the last three years (up to April 1993) the figures show public sector pay increasing faster than that in the private sector, this balance may already have changed.[51] In any case the overall figure hides a great deal of unevenness, with some of the lowest paid receiving barely any increases on already very low basic pay, while many managers and administrators have received substantial increases. More significantly, the long term decline of public sector pay compared with private is marked: since the early 1970s public sector pay has fallen by nearly a fifth relative to the private sector, and since the Clegg comparability awards of the early 1980s it has fallen by over 10 percent.[52]

These comparative figures are hardly likely to be improved by the public sector freeze on wages imposed at 1.5 percent for 1993-94 and now extended for a second year, and the continuing stagnation in many parts of private industry. Both government and employers are stressing the need to keep wage increases low. If they are successful, then many British workers will discover that they are becoming worse off.

The government wants to pursue a strategy of holding wages down and so will welcome such a development. But the political consequences of such a change in workers' fortunes for the first time since the late 1970s will be explosive. The second year of public sector pay freeze is a very risky strategy indeed, which is why only last June Chancellor of the Exchequer Kenneth Clarke claimed he had reservations about such a policy since it led to a 'bounce-back after the restraint. The longer you keep it on the more…the dangers become.'[53] The possibility of holding the line on wages, as the Tories did in 1993-94, but then finding more and more disputes including strikes the following year, is one which the government does not relish. Historically, pay struggles in response to pay restraint and wage freezes have often had a generalising and politicising effect on the unions. Struggles against pay freezes have frequently been successful in winning higher wage levels, at first for 'exceptional cases' but then for more and more groups of workers who follow the 'exceptions'.

Given the general decline in living standards in recent years, there will be widespread anger about further wage restraint. That in turn is likely to be compounded by the growing differences between workers' wages and those of managers and bosses. Professionals' pay has risen by 5.7 percent in the year up to April 1993, and that of managers by 6.2 percent.[54] But, although twice the increase gained by manual workers, it pales into insignificance next to the huge increases paid to company directors. Their average basic salary increased by 6.2 percent, but even this hides the extent to which top directors in particular have benefited. The average chief executive receives basic pay of £157,706, which nearly doubles to £261,327 when all the perks are taken into account. This in turn doubles again when share options, worth on average £298,320, are included.[55] The employers are continuing to reward themselves extremely generously—something which will fuel discontent about the pay freeze imposed on the rest of us.

The increase in poverty is not just caused by low wages, however, but is compounded by two other crucial factors: the level of taxation and the level of debt. The level of taxation is set to rise by £6 billion in March 1994 and £10 billion in March 1995—and this does not take into account any further tax increases in Chancellor Clarke's autumn 1993 budget. Despite successive cuts in income tax and a reduction of the top earners' rate of tax from 83 percent to 40 percent, the *overall* burden of taxation has risen under both Thatcher and Major. It has been shifted onto National Insurance contributions and onto value added tax, extended now to domestic fuel and threatened with extension to newspapers, children's clothes and even food.[56] The impact, as the tax is essentially regressive, has been to place a greater burden on the poor. Estimates of the March 1994 and 1995 increases, which also limit mortgage tax relief to 20 percent, show that the vast majority of households will lose around 2 percent of their incomes, but the lowest 10 percent of households will lose 3 percent, while the top 10 percent will lose only 1.5 percent of their incomes.[57] The regressive nature of the taxation—leaving the rich proportionately least burdened—is set to continue, leaving the vast majority feeling worse off.

The other key factor responsible for destroying the feeling of well-being so prevalent even among many workers during the 1980s is the debt hangover. This does not affect just the big companies, but also millions of households. The Thatcher years saw a gigantic expansion of personal debt. At the centre of this was the housing boom and the huge increase both in the number of mortgage holders and the levels of repayment with which they were burdened. In 1989, 29 percent of those with a mortgage were paying £3,000 a year or over, and another 21 percent were paying between £2,000 and 3,000.[58]

In 1981 the number of mortgages stood at 6.3 million. By 1991 it had risen to 9.6 million. Whereas arrears of over 12 months stood at 5,500 in 1982, they had reached 13,800 in 1989, 36,100 in 1990 and a staggering 59,700 in 1991. Arrears of between six and 12 months rose from 21,500 in 1981 to 66,800 in 1989, 123,100 in 1990 and 162,200 in 1991. Repossessions nearly trebled between 1989 and 1990 to 43,900.[59]

Housing debt was the largest but by no means the only area of debt. Workers were encouraged to borrow with very little restraint through the boom years of the 1980s. This made it seem as if their pay levels were actually considerably higher than they were, as credit cards took the 'waiting out of wanting'. In contrast the effect of the 'debt hangover' is to make their *actual* wage levels today lower than they might at first seem. Total personal sector debt trebled between 1980 and 1992, from £100 billion to £300 billion. 'As a percentage of total disposable income, personal-sector debt rose from less than half in 1980 to more than disposable income in 1990.'[60] Nor have most workers managed to repay much debt. Indeed, one report recently claimed that 'the proportion of consumers getting into debt rose in the second quarter [of 1993]'.[61] Levels of debt have only turned down very slightly in the depth of the recession, suggesting the costs of servicing the debts make it impossible to pay them off in full. This often leads to new debt being taken on.

No wonder any comfortable feeling of well being has disappeared.

The changed political climate

It is hard to overestimate the change in political mood which has taken place since Thatcher's heyday. At root is the change in the economy: economic expansion, skill shortages in many areas, boom industries in many parts of the country, rising property prices which gave those workers with mortgages a sense of growing prosperity, rising real incomes, all contributed to the complacency of the mid to late 1980s. Those who worried about riots, rising crime, homelessness, or the decline of health and education provision were told that these problems would be solved as the free market took hold. The wealth generated by companies and rich individuals would eventually 'trickle down' to everyone. But the rich had to be allowed to get richer, public spending had to continue being reined back, otherwise the magical forces of the market would not be able to work.

This view was always only rather grudgingly and partially accepted by most workers. Thatcherism has been described as being 'hegemonic' during the 1980s, suggesting a positive and enthusiastic endorsement of Thatcherite values by millions of workers. This was never the case. Electorally, the Tories remained a minority party throughout the decade. Politically, the grasping, selfish, yuppie values associated with the creed never permeated to the mass of ordinary working people. So even at the height of 'Thatcherism' after the defeat of the year long miners' strike in 1985, and during the Lawson boom, most people espoused collectivist, welfarist and egalitarian attitudes over most issues. Indeed, comparisons between opinion surveys in the mid-1970s and those in 1983 and 1986 show that Thatcher's rule created a higher awareness of the social causes of poverty in the later years.[62] Labour's electoral doldrums were still mainly a result of its attacks on workers when last in government in 1974-79 and the failure of its local councils to protect people from Tory policies. Its constant moves towards Tory ground did not help. And Thatcher could not have won most of her victories without a degree of treachery from within the workers' movement itself. The miners' strike could not have been defeated without the splits in the Labour Party and TUC over the strike. Rupert Murdoch could not have moved to Wapping and smashed the print unions without the willingness of the electricians' union to recruit scabs. And when the attacks on the NHS became obvious in 1988, there was a national wave of sympathy for the striking Manchester nurses which forced the government onto the defensive—a position it has occupied ever since.

Once the boom began to come to an end, even the superficial gains which most workers had made during the Thatcher years looked less attractive. The residue left after the tide went out included record debt, millions with mortgages they could not afford—often on houses whose value fell far lower than the value of the mortgage itself—the decline of overtime, bonuses and other opportunities to augment salaries whose basic levels were quite low. On top of this was the continuing decline in the public sector: transport, hospitals, libraries—and, perhaps most important, the looming threat of unemployment.

The sense of betrayal felt by millions during the recession has been tangible. Workers were cajoled, persuaded and bribed into buying houses, using easy credit to buy cars, holidays and furniture, on the assumption that the good times would never come to an end. Then they did. The economy ran out of control, and could not slow down gradually. Instead it crashed to a halt. This reversal of fortunes was part of what led to a change in attitudes. But the common assumption, even by some on the left, that hostility to government and other changes in attitudes are simply the product of workers being directly hit in the pocket is false. If we look more closely at the changes in attitudes which have taken place, they clearly stem from a much broader and deeper disaffection with society.

It is true that many people are centrally concerned about one question; whether their jobs are safe. Despite a fall in total unemployment for a few months in the spring and summer of 1993, the number of people who feared they would be thrown on the dole grew. For example, in August 1993, 47 percent of those asked said they were very or fairly con- cerned about losing their job.[63] The same survey demonstrated that between April and August 1993 the number of people aged under 24 who worried about redundancy and unemployment rose from 40 percent to 50 percent. The number of unskilled and semi-skilled manual workers concerned about the dole rose from 44 to 53 percent. But we should remember that fear of unemployment is not something limited to the 'down' side of the business cycle. Mass unemployment, varying between the historically high levels of 1 million and 3 million, has haunted British society for 20 years. That fear has been translated into hatred of a government which has presided over unemployment.

Attitudes on other issues have also shifted. So another poll, conducted in September 1993, showed that 77 percent thought that 'there is one law for the rich and one for the poor.' Only 18 percent favoured privatisation, and 46 percent thought that 'more socialist planning would be the best way to solve Britain's economic problems'—including 24 percent of Tory voters questioned.[64] Polls on taxation show a similar change in atti- tudes. Not only do a clear majority favour increasing taxes rather than cutting public spending, they also favour increasing the higher rate of tax. In a recent poll 59 percent wanted the higher rate raised, compared with 41 percent wanting the basic rate raised and only 14 percent wanting higher VAT. The most popular area for cuts was defence spending, with 64 percent in favour. Even cuts in social security benefit—the favourite Tory scapegoat—were only favoured by 31 percent of those questioned.[65]

Perhaps even greater changes of attitudes have taken place in areas which cannot be considered narrowly economic. Education—long an area where the left has been on the defensive and a small band of right wingers have been making the running—has become an arena where the right has found itself totally isolated. A recent poll showed that 73 percent of those polled thought league tables were 'damaging' and 83 percent were against moving teacher training to classrooms. Testing at seven years old was thought unnecessary by 66 percent.[66]

A similar change in attitudes has undermined the sorts of institutions which most people believe are central to any sort of consensus in British politics: parliament, the judiciary, the police, the monarchy. Respect for such institutions seems to be at an all time low. A recent poll in the *Financial Times* showed that the institutions most perceived to have improved between 1992 and 1993 were the supermarkets, while those seen to have got worse included prisons, law courts, the police, hospitals, transport, job centres and social security offices.[67]

The justice system is widely perceived as being corrupt and unfair. The Birmingham Six, the Guildford Four and the Judith Ward case are just three of the Irish cases which have undermined popular faith in the police and the judiciary. But it is clear that rottenness and corruption of the system extends to many supposedly non-political cases such as the M25 Three or the Taylor Sisters. And Winston Silcott languishes in jail despite being cleared of the killing of PC Blakelock.

The monarchy has been badly tarnished by the successive royal scandals, the queen's grudging and belated agreement to pay some tax and the monarchy's demand that the taxpayer foot the bill for repairing the fire damage at Windsor Castle. Parliament is seen as full of politicians on the make. By 1991, fewer people expressed public confidence in the police, legal system, education, parliament, the church, the civil service and the press than had done so in 1981. The only two areas which attracted higher public confidence in 1991 than ten years previously were the armed forces and the trade unions.[68]

The employers' offensive

The employers were as surprised as anyone when boom turned to recession. True there had been agonising since 1988 about what would happen to the economy. How would the overheating of the economy develop? Would there be a soft landing or a hard landing? Were company assets over-valued? But these were a minority of worried voices. Most employers just got on with making the most of the good times. They responded to the speed and severity of recession in the traditional way: in addition to plant closures and job losses they attempted wage cuts or freezes, lay offs and attacks on conditions. Large numbers of workers suffered attempts to reduce or abolish tea breaks and benefits, and, in some places, to impose temporary contracts on new workers. Everywhere the recession was used as a means of trying to worsen workers' conditions and to tilt the balance between workers and employers in favour of the latter.

By 1990 such incursions were well under way. However, despite the pessimism of the trade union leaders that fear of unemployment would frighten anyone who even thought about fighting back, these attacks met with opposition, although of varying degrees of intensity and success. An attempt to restructure working patterns at Rolls-Royce was rolled back by the threat of action. Shipyard workers at Yarrow's in Glasgow managed to stop new workers being taken on at a lower rate.[69] The effect of recession on different industries and groups of workers was uneven. So pay increases still tended to be in double figures (compared with 1993 they seem astronomical), with 12 to 13 percent at Ford and Vauxhall,[70] and 12.5 percent offered at Jaguar, Coventry (a figure narrowly accepted, with two fifths of workers against the deal).[71] It was as though the employers were willing to pay for industrial peace so that they could squeeze the last drops of profit out of the boom. They were also still suffering from one of the features of late 1980s expansion— skill shortages. Although overall jobs were being lost, the shortage of skills was still acute in certain industries. So, for example, in late 1990 some British Rail signals staff won 25 percent wage increases in order to keep their skills in the industry.[72] But the picture was very uneven. At the same time, there were moves towards wage cuts.[73]

The past three years have been characterised, however, by a remarkable failure on the part of the employers to really use the recession to attack workers' organisation *on the scale that they would like*. The period has seen employers move onto the offensive, encounter at least verbal opposition, and very often make at least some tactical retreat rather than move into full confrontation with their workforce. This outcome is all the more remarkable given the general nature of the attacks. It was commonplace early in the recession to argue that this was a 'services recession' and that manufacturing industry would not be so badly hit. In reality the slump has affected every area of industry, and the attacks on wages and conditions have applied across both the private and the public sectors, creating a situation whereby today no worker (and indeed no member of lower or middle management) feels secure in his or her job, and where every worker is facing threats of change in working conditions.

The generalised nature of the attacks is one reason why the political mood is so volatile and angry. The attacks have tended to have a contradictory effect. The whole point of privatisation, market testing in the civil service, or indeed 'rationalisation programmes' in the private sector has been to cut jobs, raise levels of productivity and introduce 'flexibility' within the particular workforce. There have been two simultaneous reactions to this. The first is a sense of demoralisation and weakening of workers' organisation, as shop stewards find their position under attack and workers find 'custom and practice' undermined. Such feelings of demoralisation tend to play into the employers' hands. At the same time the attacks can have the opposite effect. So there can be an increased level of fightback, as the employers' offensive forces often previously passive and 'moderate' groups of workers into action.

Even groups of workers such as college lecturers, who only two decades ago would have hardly considered themselves as trade unionists, are now turning to militant action, including strikes, as the only means of defending their conditions. The motivation is simple: from relatively privileged conditions compared with many workers (short hours, reasonable working conditions and above average pay) they find themselves subject to downward pressure on wages, and speed up at work—increased through-put of students, longer hours, shorter holidays, administrative burdens on top of teaching work. Some of the old attitudes still linger, but they increasingly see their work as little different from routine clerical work. Teachers are suffering the same sorts of pressure, with their work becoming harder and less valued. The boycott of school tests received almost total support from teachers (and even head teachers), reflecting both the accumulation of years of bitterness at worsening conditions, and a feeling that the only way of stopping the attacks is through industrial action.

The view of the trade union leaders and many in the media that 'workers won't fight in a recession' has been shown to be very wide of the mark. The past three years have seen a willingness to fight over pay, jobs and conditions. Sometimes the levels of anger have expressed themselves in struggles over non-economic issues, such as the 1,500 strong Oxford post office workers' strike in opposition to sexual harassment of a female worker by a supervisor.[74] However, it is also true that these strikes have not led to a generalised fightback, or to any qualitative change in the industrial struggle over the past three years. Why has that been the case, and how can we overcome the weaknesses of the movement?

What is the nature of the fightback?

A pattern has emerged in recent years. Attacks take place on workers from government and private sector employers. The scale of the attack provokes in nearly every case real resentment and opposition. The workers concerned protest. They stage ballots, lobbies and one day strikes. At every stage the union leaders will reflect this anger only in the most passive and obsequious way. They caution against strikes, rush to compromise with the employers (sometimes before any real concession is made), and do their utmost to restrict the action to the most token and limited kind. The outcome is usually, therefore, at best compromise, at worst sell out which results in defeat for the workers concerned, who in turn face victimisation and demoralisation.

Time and again the picture of the disputes during the last three years is one of false starts, militant feeling and often a real urge for action which is frittered away by months of balloting and negotiations. We can see this early in the recession in disputes such as the long running Greenwich housing workers' strike, or the strike by British Rail guards at Manchester Piccadilly in the autumn of 1990. TUC leader Norman Willis stated in January 1991 that 'now is not the time for class warriors on either side to be locked into an historic conflict over allocation of fast disappearing spoils which will destroy their own and their colleagues' jobs'.[75] Such views have remained the watchwords of the union leaders right through the recession years.

Yet the seemingly unfavourable circumstances existing in the first half of 1991—steeply accelerating job losses and deepening recession against the background of the Gulf War—did not stop many groups of workers from disregarding Willis's advice. The main impetus for many of these strikes was employers raising the stakes in one way or another—imposing cuts in jobs, victimising shop stewards and union activists, changing rotas and shift patterns to squeeze more work out of the work-force. But the strikes very often showed a militancy and involvement which took them beyond the purely defensive. A strike at Glasgow's Queen Street station over management attacks on guards led to a partial victory for the workers. In the same week, in January 1991, 2,000 Tower Hamlets council workers staged a one day strike against victimisation, there were votes to strike at GM buses in Manchester over the sacking of a union chair, and Southwark council workers voted to strike against the cuts.[76]

By March and April 1991 the stage was set for bigger confrontations. Rail and tube workers, members of the RMT union, were set for a fight over job cuts. There was every sign that the fight over pay would take off among a wide range of workers: there were the possibilities of battles in health, power, steel and the BBC.[77] In May the tube workers' ballot—overwhelmingly in favour of strike—was announced, and at the same time textile workers, post office counter staff and rail workers were bal-loting over pay.[78]

There were signs that the militant and successful strikes over govern-ment pay policy in the summer of 1989 could be repeated. A mini strike wave in the north east of England took place as 600 ship repairers at

Appledore's struck over pay and were sacked, 1,500 Tyneside bus drivers struck over pay, AEI Cables workers in Gateshead joined an indefinite pay strike and 1,000 Teesside British Steel workers rejected a 4 percent pay offer.[79] In Glasgow 1,600 Kvaerner Govan shipyard workers walked out *against the advice of their officials and shop stewards* over pay and shift changes.[80] Perhaps most remarkable, not in terms of industrial action but in demonstration of the change of mood since the mid-1980s, workers at Rupert Murdoch's Wapping plant voted six to one for action 'short of a strike' and printers held up production in protest at redundancies and new shift patterns.[81]

The mood was certainly not for surrendering to the employers' demands. Indeed, a much more common feeling was that the recession was the fault of government and employers and that they should pay for it. The mood continued into the summer, when bus workers from the London Forest company came out on indefinite strike against pay cuts and changed working conditions.[82] But none of the strikes succeeded in marking a wider breakthrough, although many of them ended in at least a partial victory. Throughout the union leaders were for compromise and retreat. They increasingly used the imminent election as an argument against direct action. So at the NALGO and COHSE union conferences that year the key argument was that defence of the NHS had to wait for a Labour government.[83]

A combination of union leaders' reluctance to take the struggle forward, and the employers backing off when faced with the threat of or some limited industrial action meant the promise of action was not fulfilled. Sometimes too the employers just dug their heels in and sat out long strikes, such as those at Albacom and Craven Tasker in Scotland. By the autumn of 1991 there were signs that this sort of confrontation with the employers was becoming more of a pattern. For example, in engineering there were disputes at the two workplaces mentioned plus Unipart, Perkins Diesels and Marston.[84]

The prospect of an approaching election made the union leaders more cautious than usual, with the AEU hailing a single-union deal with Toyota,[85] which conceded a 39 hour working week at a time when most major engineering plants had won 37 hours. GMB leader John Edmonds declared that the Tories would use 'industrial trouble as a desperate election ploy'.[86] In the last months of 1991 and the first months of 1992 the level of struggle was low, with just a handful of often very long and bitterly fought strikes, such as the dispute at the *Rotherham Advertiser* over union derecognition, and the militant but ultimately defeated strike at Manchester's GEC Alsthom plant against compulsory redundancies.[87]

The mood to 'wait for Labour' played a great part in ensuring that industrial struggle remained muted, although there were strikes and demonstrations against local government cuts, and strike ballots on the

London underground over job losses, among Barclays Bank workers over pay, and at Blue Circle Cement against a pay freeze.[88]

The election result itself destroyed the 'wait for Labour' argument in one blow. Although it caused further demoralisation to tens of thousands of activists, the sense of shock and bewilderment which greeted the Tory victory did not last for very long. Within three months of the election, there had been a sharp change of mood reflected not necessarily in the number of struggles but in their militancy and intensity, and in the sense of crisis already facing the Major government. Waves of protest at the cuts in education, health and council services swept London in the summer of 1992. The mood of anger was created by a further sense of betrayal among those, some of whom had voted Tory in April, suffering from further job losses and cuts. *Socialist Worker*'s headline of 20 June summed it up: 'Major's big lie: slump continues, record dole queues, savage new cuts'.[89]

Black Wednesday dramatically increased the sense of tension. Sackings were continuing inexorably—with 3,000 jobs going at British Aerospace and 1,500 at Ford—when the announcement over pit closures on 13 October brought to a head all the resentment and anger into one giant protest which threatened to bring down the government just six months after its election.

In every workplace in every local community all but the most diehard right wingers were horrified at plans to destroy what was left of the coal industry. Local demonstrations in support of the miners and two gigantic marches in London attracted near universal support. Talk of general strike was on the lips of people who had voted Tory the previous April. John Major's personal unpopularity now exceeded that of Thatcher. The movement round the miners saw the resurgence of a level of generalised working class consciousness which had not been seen for many years. The weekday demonstration called by the miners and their supporters in central London attracted sizeable contingents of workers from every city in the country. There was sporadic strike action, especially where local militants argued for it, even though this was discouraged by the trade union leaders. Delegations came from post offices, fire stations, construction sites, from Ford and Vauxhall, Rolls-Royce, Rover Longbridge, from rail depots, hospitals, schools and council offices.[90]

The movement around the miners created a feeling of confidence among workers generally. At the end of October *Daily Mirror* journalists occupied their newsroom in protest at the appointment of union buster David Montgomery. Newham council workers went back on all out strike in their long running dispute over sackings. Workers staged a brief occupation of their ice cream factory against closure in Kirkby, Merseyside.[91] The Tories were completely taken aback and fearful that the protests could spread to industrial action elsewhere, hence their U-turn intended to take the sting out of the controversy. The announcement that the queen would agree to pay tax followed shortly afterwards, as they tried desperately to shore up support and appease some of those who increasingly realised that their society was based on class inequality.

Perhaps most important, however, was the role of the union leaders themselves, both in taking control of the movement and in trying to deflect it into lobbying, 'broad' popular front campaigns with Tory MPs, and away from any notion of industrial action. Crucially they prevented other workers from taking the sort of action which could build the growing opposition to the government. So Jimmy Knapp, leader of the RMT union, called off the tube workers' strike—after *three* votes for action—on the grounds that there was no real mood for a strike![92]

As a result the pits campaign had really lost its momentum by the time, months later, that Heseltine produced his 'reprieve' for some of the pits. The trade union leaders and the Labour Party gave the government time, and it used the time to defuse the anger, make minor concessions, and claim that the 'free market' (actually a market totally rigged in favour of gas and nuclear power), not the government, was forcing the closures through. The outcome of the TUC strategy has been disaster: all the 31 originally threatened pits will close and probably more besides. The much vaunted Tory rebellion eventually amounted to five MPs, a year after the original closure announcement had provoked so much anger.[93] This represents a complete frittering away of the biggest mass campaign for years by the leaders of the working class movement.

We can see the same picture in microcosm in a whole number of the disputes which broke out during 1993. These have been characterised by higher levels of bitterness even than those of the previous summer, let alone those before the election. There is more of a sense that it is better to fight and be defeated than do nothing, since the advantage of doing nothing becomes less and less when jobs are going on such a massive scale, and when so many workers are having to work harder for less money. Two disputes in particular reflect this mood. Timex workers in Dundee (mostly women) refused to accept worsened conditions imposed on them by management and struck. They preferred to see the factory close (the eventual outcome) than to see the union broken and workers in Dundee forced onto worse conditions. The huge support for their lengthy strike demonstrated how many other workers agreed with them. But the failure of the strike to move beyond picketing to winning blacking from other British Timex plants (illegal under the anti-union laws and therefore expressly forbidden by the engineering union leaders) meant they were never able to really deal a body blow to the company.

The strike by nurses at University College Hospital, London, against closure again attracted huge levels of (albeit more localised) support. The nurses struck knowing that the alternative would be job losses anyway. The six week strike was an incredible achievement given the lack of health service tradition over all out strike action, and the luke-warm support from the nurses' union, UNISON. But in the end the relatively small scale strike, popular as it was, could not overcome the lack of action elsewhere and UNISON's failure to give it full support, finally pulling the plug on finance for the dispute. The nurses went back with management agreeing not to discipline the strike's leaders. Yet both strikes demonstrate the lengths to which workers are prepared to go, and the anger that such disputes represent.

How can we sum up the events of the class struggle in the past few years? The majority of disputes have been characterised by extreme bit-terness. This has become more marked over the past year. The mood after the election has been quite different from what went before.

This, obviously, is a subjective view. There is no easy way of mea-suring why workers do or do not strike. And the strike figures certainly show a very low level of strike activity. In 1991 there were 800,000 days 'lost' through industrial disputes, supposedly the lowest figure for 100 years. But they were also very low in 1976, in 1981-83 and in 1986-87. The number of stoppages is also the lowest for 50 years, although, as the government statisticians themselves admit, 'small stoppages involving fewer than ten workers or lasting less than one day are excluded from the statistics...disputes not resulting in a stoppage of work are not included in the statistics.'[94]

What we learn from the figures therefore is that there is little mood among the official leaders to call disputes (unlike the two high points of strike days in recent years, the 1979 Winter of Discontent and the 1984-85 miners' strike). Nor is there a mood of militancy among workers sufficient to see the figures climb without the blessing of the union offi-cials. But the figures do not tell us much more.

Most important of all, it is impossible to judge the political situation simply by reference to the strike figures or even the industrial struggle alone. There are several other factors to take into account. Firstly, there are a number of strikes balloted for successfully which simply do not take place—usually because the employers make some concessions and the union leaders accept a compromise. There are some disputes which do not even get to the final strike ballot—the dispute of the firefighters, in the summer and autumn of 1993 over the retention of their pay formula would not show up in any of these figures. Half day strikes over cuts, or walkouts in support of the miners, or that of the council workers in the Isle of Dogs in protest at the election of a fascist councillor, would similarly be ignored.

Secondly, much of the industrial action which does take place is restricted to one day strikes at most. There have been very large numbers of these over the past three years—by council workers in various parts of the country, by teachers (for example Islington teachers staged three one day strikes in the summer of 1992 against compulsory redundancies),[95] by London bus workers, and by rail workers. Very often they attract overwhelming support and high levels of militancy. The Islington teachers voted 85 percent for strike action on a 92 percent turnout, for example. But, because the strikes are restricted to one day affairs, they very often do not have a lasting impact on the consciousness of the workers themselves or on other workers.

The third feature of the disputes which never surfaces in the statistics is the growing anger and disgust of a minority of those involved with the sell outs of the trade union leaders. In every dispute a minority sees through the dominant strategy and wants to do something more. Although this minority is not usually sufficient to alter the balance of forces, it makes it harder for the union leaders to get their own way. One important example of this was the UCW strike in Cardiff in the summer of 1993. The strike involved high levels of militancy and solidarity from other post workers, only to be sold short by an official who was then besieged in his office by angry workers.[96]

All these factors help to paint a much more complex picture of the industrial scene than the one with which we are usually presented. And the mood of militancy extends far beyond workplace issues to embrace anger at attacks on living standards, the problems of debt, the huge increases in bosses' salaries, rising taxation under the Tories, and the rundown of the NHS. There is a substantial degree of rank and file anger which is belied by the strike figures.

Evidence of the breadth of protest is there in the demonstrations, campaigns and pickets which have occurred over a range of issues in recent years. The opposition to what is happening to the NHS has extended far beyond those directly working in the health service, with huge levels of support from other workers. There have been militant protests at the siting of yet more superstores on greenfield sites. The attempt to stop a motorway through the Hampshire beauty spot of Twyford Down failed, but not before direct action required injunctions to stop the protesters. As the result of a similar protest, plans to drive a motorway through ancient woodland in south east London were abandoned, and there have been continuing demonstrations to stop the bulldozers demolishing houses in east London for the M11 link road. Every city and many towns in Britain can point to similar grass roots resistance.

Protesters over job losses, schools cuts and environmental damage have been joined by campaigners against VAT on fuel. Largely led by pensioners, who have demonstrated and lobbied repeatedly against this iniquitous tax increase, it is likely to become one of the biggest issues facing the Major government in 1994.

The British National Party election victory in September 1993 raised the political temperature in Britain considerably. The size of opposition to the fascists was demonstrated in the Unity demonstration in Welling the following month, when nearly 600 coaches helped to bring 60,000 people from every corner of the country to demand the closure of the BNP's headquarters.

Given the high level of politicisation in Britain today, large numbers of people are drawing the connections between these different issues. Unfortunately they are given little leadership or direction from those at the head of the labour movement.

Softly, softly: the Labour and trade union leaders

The Thatcher and Major years have revealed a crisis of Labourism. The worst phase of this crisis was during the early 1980s when Thatcher's second election victory led to a sharp shift to the right under Neil Kinnock, then the party's new leader. This move to the right has continued in the decade since, with the gradual abandonment of every major policy on which Labour stood in the early 1980s. By the 1992 election any idea of Labour as a party committed to radical change had all but disappeared, as its policy accepted more and more of the Tory ground on economic strategy, unemployment, defence and foreign policy and privatisation.

> *Of the four pillars of the post-war settlement—counter-cyclical demand management, mixed economy, full employment, welfare state—only the last remained inviolate. Its improvement, however, depended upon the economic growth expected from an orthodox liberal managerial posture, aided by the ERM, in conjunction with a long term industrial strategy whose harvest was, by definition, for the future. 'Supply-side socialism' was, in effect, what one observer dubbed a 'left Heseltinism'.*[97]

After the 1992 defeat even the welfare state has been less than inviolate. So Labour's 'modernisers' are moving away from ideas of collective provision such as universal benefits, using the excuse that many people no longer need them, or that they subsidise the middle classes. They have also moved away from their traditional economic mixture of high taxation and high public spending. The Commission on Social Justice, set up by John Smith in January 1993 to 'think the unthinkable' about the future of the welfare state, is engaged in producing new Labour policies which will almost certainly concede many Tory arguments. Labour's ambition to run a more modern, efficient British capitalism, regardless of the cost to workers, is clear.

Labour's move rightwards has not been without a price. It has suffered internal conflict, including expulsion of many left wing activists and repeated faction fights within the party, but has come little closer to achieving parliamentary power. Labour's lead in the opinion polls, which was beginning to evaporate as early as September 1991, disappeared completely on polling day itself. This led to Kinnock's departure, and the conclusion by the bulk of Labour's membership, as well as its leaders, that Labour had to further 'modernise'—loosen its links with the unions and appeal to the middle classes who, the story goes, were put off by fears of higher taxation under Labour.

To date this strategy has had little success. Labour is ahead in the opinion polls—but there would be something badly wrong if it were not, given the record unpopularity of the Tories. November 1993 figures put Labour at between 40 and 45 percent, not exactly an overwhelming endorsement.[98] Labour's lack of differentiation from the other parties means that it still does not seem a sufficiently distinct alternative. Its record in local government—it now has the largest number of local government seats—of cuts, redundancies, and jailings over the poll tax has also helped tarnish its image.

The Labour Party also has huge internal problems. Labour is withering at its roots, a recent survey shows. Its activists are deserting in droves, its membership shrinking fast, and there is no obvious sign of how this trend can be reversed. Nearly 7,000 Labour Party members contributed to the survey by Patrick Seyd and Paul Whiteley which shows deep disaffection among Labour activists and a sharp decline in activism. For example, 'in 1990, 82 percent of members had been involved in some form of party campaign in the previous year, whereas by 1992 only 56 percent had.' Less people were delivering leaflets, canvassing and attending meetings by 1992; the only activity which had increased was giving money. Former members questioned about why they had left revealed a quarter quit because Labour abandoned basic principles or moved too far to the right. A further quarter mentioned specific policies, particularly Labour's support for the Gulf War.[99]

These findings are very serious for Labour, although perhaps not surprising for many active on the left in Britain, as Labour's lack of inspiration, willingness to fight and its attacks on activists has left its members disoriented, demoralised and passive. It is in danger of becoming an increasingly old party with a smaller and smaller membership, a finding which the survey's authors say means that 'the activists are a diminishing number, and Labour could thus become a parliamentary head with no roots'.[100]

The lack of concern felt by much of Labour's leadership for these sorts of problems has led to the divisions expressed during the past year between Labour's 'modernisers' and 'traditionalists'. This is not obviously a clear left-right split, since most of the protagonists are still hostile to the far left, and since even in the traditionally left wing constituency parties there has clearly been a sharp rightward shift.[101] Instead it reflects a feeling that the 'modernising' changes are threatening the whole basis of Labour as a party capable of delivering any reforms and making it indistinguishable from the Tories. Talk of leapfrogging over the Tories often leads some shadow cabinet members closer to the Tory *right* than to its left wing, as Ian Aitken, by no means a Labour left winger, has pointed out:

> We have the remarkable spectacle of the post-Thatcherite Tory party riven from top to bottom over exactly the question at issue—namely, whether to raise taxes in order to maintain effective services, or cut services in order to maintain low taxes. Yet Mr Brown has chosen this very moment to attach himself, however tentatively, to the right wing side of the argument.[102]

The same sort of fear appears in the debate on the link between the unions and Labour, with some thinking that one member one vote will throw the baby out with the bathwater and leave Labour weaker, not stronger. Peter Hain, the 'soft left' MP for Neath, has argued that:

> To win, a party must first motivate its members, its potential recruits and its core voters. That will not be sufficient but it is an essential precondition for victory. By such a test, the modernisers are failing badly. The steady demor-alisation of the party's membership has accelerated with every modernising lurch—and is now almost terminal.[103]

The message put across by Hain and those union leaders such as Bill Morris and John Edmonds who led the fight against one member one vote (the attempt to substitute individual votes in constituencies for any collective trade union input) at Labour's conference is that leapfrogging has gone too far. The 'modernisation' of Labour's 1992 election campaign left it with a vote barely higher than the two previous elections, but with a much smaller and more demoralised membership. Yet the 'traditionalists' are denounced as old fashioned, even though it is much more likely that they reflect a feeling of discontent among Labour and trade union activists. A typical expression of this mood—not from hard left wingers who have in large part been driven out of the party, but from the centre left of the party—came from a Labour member in Norwich, a large, active 'traditional' party:

> It's absolute bollocks to say the electorate doesn't want us to retain those links [with the unions]. I've done about 50 meetings on the subject around the south [of England], and everyone thinks the present constitutional debate is an irrelevance. People are more concerned about the health service, educa-

tion and crime. It's a media myth, and I think I represent the mainstream in that view.[104]

The narrow vote which eventually brought the modernisers victory at Labour's 1993 conference in the move towards one member one vote has not resolved this tension. John Smith was forced to make concessions towards the importance of the unions, both at the TUC's own congress and at Labour Party conference itself, in order to win the votes of a whole number of affiliated unions. Indeed, Smith claimed the move would strengthen the link between the party and the unions in his conference speech.[105] He could not win without reaffirming some of the 'traditional values' of Labour. He, along with his shadow chancellor, Gordon Brown, then seemed to distance themselves from arch moderniser Tony Blair.[106]And the media, having demanded the vote, then claimed that Labour was still in hock to the unions and that little had changed, thus negating the point of changing the voting system anyway.

The argument over one member one vote is symptomatic of Labour's problems. Like the generals in the First World War it is continually fighting the battles of the previous war. Its changes are therefore either too little too late, and denounced by the media as brought about grudgingly or the changes fail to match the mood of the public opinion the leadership is so desperate to chase. The decline in its active membership leads Labour into a vicious circle. The leaders are more and more out of touch, and in many parts of the country—especially the south of England—have effectively written off the possibility of victory. There are fewer and fewer active members in these areas to campaign and argue with potential voters, so the whole place is abandoned to the Liberals. Liberal victory is then in turn hailed as evidence that Labour cannot win. It will take more than conference debate to shake the Labour leadership from this course. It will require events outside the narrow world of parliamentary party politics to push Labour in another direction.

What of the union leaders? Despite their often bitter differences over how much they influence Labour policy, and their justifiable resentment at the idea that the unions lost Labour the 1992 election, they have no serious alternative strategy. Labour's leadership may be reluctant to endorse any industrial action, but the union leaders themselves are hardly more enthusiastic. The head of the TUC, John Monks, said recently that calls for days of strike action were 'simplistic'. At a time when a TUC commissioned poll found that nearly eight out of ten people thought trade unions were necessary to protect workers' interests, Monks declared:

The job of unions is to avoid strikes, particularly ones of any duration. There is often an initial enthusiasm among workers when they embark on industrial action. But during strikes income is lost, job security threatened and people are vulnerable to victimisation. Strikes can be necessary against bad employers, but they are a weapon of last resort.[107]

In evidence to the House of Commons employment committee the TUC outlined its strategy of worker-employer participation to strengthen British capitalism: unions can help competitiveness, and collective bargaining can lead to smoother workplace relations. As the *Financial Times* reported, 'the TUC denies any inherent conflict between capital and labour in the workplace.' The TUC document argues that 'it does not follow that trade unionists are less committed to their company than other employees.'[108] There is no sign that most of the trade union leaders differ in any crucial respect from this view. So, despite angry words when the government announced a second year of public sector wage freeze last September, they rapidly retreated from any notion of strike action. John Edmonds argued that 'the chancellor's pay freeze is an attempt to trap public sector workers into a strike and to take the spotlight off his own difficulties', while the TGWU's Jack Dromey declared that 'it is clear that part of the government's agenda is to trap us and thereby trap the Labour Party'.[109]

This approach has dominated the union leaders' attitude to industrial action throughout the Major years. They argue that such action is outdated, and that the successive legal constraints passed by the Tories prevent strikes being successful. There is no doubting the effect of the law on disputes. The engineering union officials and Scottish TUC successfully argued against mass picketing and blacking of goods in the Timex dispute. There are countless examples where action has been prevented because the union officials claim it is illegal and will bankrupt the union.

Yet although the union leaders portray themselves as the helpless victims of the law, there is some evidence that they use the law as a shield to hide their own lack of militancy. It is quite clear that the main function of the anti-union laws is to reinforce the union leaders' own caution and conservatism, and that most of the time, even when there is not much industrial action involved, the laws remain paper tigers. A London School of Economics survey of negotiators from 25 trade unions, representing over 5 million workers, found widespread support among them for pre-strike ballots, with 68 percent finding them 'a good thing for trade unions'. The survey also found that employers were reluctant to use the law. It says that 'legal proceedings—or even a solicitor's letter—are still clearly the exception'. Only a quarter of those questioned said employers had threatened to use the law over industrial action—and only a quarter of these (ie just one-sixteenth of the total) had even begun legal proceedings.[110]

So the real picture is that employers are still loathe to use the law in industrial disputes—luckily for them the officials' reluctance to call action means they are not often faced with the choice. Time and again in the past three years they have claimed there was not the support for action or that proposed action was illegal. Even when officials have wanted some limited action they are so fearful of the law that they refuse to call it directly, instead couching their language in veiled hints which do not help to mobilise. In particular, they keep any disputes which do break out as narrowly based as possible, refusing to call any solidarity action which is, of course, illegal. This was most apparent round the miners in October and November 1992, when solidarity strikes were rejected as a strategy, and replaced by one of winning public opinion and lobbying dissident Tories.

The right wing of the movement was enthusiastic about this strategy; if the left was less so, it raised no public opposition. Even Arthur Scargill went along with the TUC's campaign uncritically, at least in public. Claiming that he would act when the time was right, he attacked those (such as the Socialist Workers Party) who argued in November and December for occupations of the pits in order to escalate the campaign.[111]

However, it would be wrong to assume that the only reason for lack of militancy inside the working class is the conservatism of the trade union leaders. If this were the case, it would be relatively easy to sweep them out of the way on a tide of militant generalised struggle. But the picture is much more complicated than this. There are many instances when the rank and file does not fight, even when the union leaders urge action. An analysis of why there is not more militancy has to take account of the working class movement *as a whole*. How do we explain it?

The feeling among the trade union leaders does not exist in isolation at the top of the movement, but rests on and is reflected by a whole layer of shop stewards, convenors, trade union branch secretaries and trades council activists. They hate what is happening to them at work, the weakening of the unions and the attacks on the welfare state. They feel that something has to be done to roll back these attacks. But they are the victims of the Thatcher and Major years—and even of the Callaghan Labour government before them. The downturn in class struggle during those years, the successive defeat of strong groups of workers such as the miners and print workers, has left them with a sense of powerlessness. They feel that very little can be done to change things, and that the only hope is the election of a Labour government. They are not even optimistic about that. They reflect a strong element of pessimism and cynicism, caused partly by the national union leaders who they feel are out of touch with them and with ordinary workers. But they are also sceptical about the ability of ordinary workers to fight after years of accepting Tory attacks.

Yet this pessimism jostles side by side with more militant ideas even in the mind of a single individual: these are the activists who, for example, reflected a much higher level of militancy at the union conferences in the spring and summer of 1993, but at the same time feel that they cannot carry industrial action in the health service or fire brigade. This pessimism reflects the attitudes of the Labour and trade union leaders, with the assumption that direct action never works and that all that can be done is to rely on voting to change things. This in turn leads to passivity among many workers which itself reinforces the same reformist conclusions.

In every dispute or strike all sorts of different ideas and considerations are in competition for the allegiance of those involved. Anger at a particular grievance, a deep sense of injustice as custom and practice are unilaterally varied, the erosion of wage levels and living standards, all create motivation for action. But there is always fear and hesitation at the same time: will there be victimisations or sackings, is it worth striking for the money involved, can anything be gained from an intransigent government or employer? Here the subjective question of confidence, of experience of strikes, of some assessment of the balance of forces, is vitally important.

In this sense the role of leadership is particularly important today. Even though the picture is not simply that the leaders hold back the members, it is true that the conservatism of the union leaders is very often strongly in contrast with the militants who get involved in disputes. So, even where there is a fight, the union leaders can influence levels of confidence and militancy. But so can organised socialists. The fact that this fine balance between fightback and retreat exists is the great change since the 1980s—and a great challenge for the left.

The future in the present

Writing in this journal 15 years ago, Tony Cliff explained why the working class movement had gone into decline from the mid-1970s. He explained the erosion of rank and file workers' organisation of shop stewards, and the limitations of industrial militancy in a period of economic and political crisis. The early 1970s had seen a workers' industrial offensive on the one hand and political generalisation by the employers on the other:

*The unstable balance between the political generalisation on the employers'
side and the industrial militancy on the workers' side could lead to one of two*

extremes: to political generalisation of the industrial militancy, or to the decline of sectional militancy. The latter took place as a result of the misleadership of the trade union bureaucracy, the Labour left and the Communist Party.[112]

With the onset of economic crisis, politics are absolutely central to leadership inside the workers' movement:

[the crisis] *cannot be met with the weapons of yesteryear. Such fragmented reaction will not do now, on the wages front, not to say on the front of cuts, closures and unemployment. The muddled thinking of workers in the years of the boom did not prevent them from still improving their material conditions. Now what happens in the grey matter of workers' heads is decisive for their material well-being. Politics, socialist politics, has therefore to be brought to the shop floor.*[113]

Then the movement faced a turning point between decline and advance. The failure of the movement as a whole to learn the correct lessons from the disputes led to a whole series of defeats during the 1980s. Now we face another turning point between further decline or revival. In both cases socialist politics are vital.

The struggles of the Major years have only reinforced the analysis outlined above. Since it was written we have seen two recessions and a boom which delivered little permanent improvement in the living standards of most workers. The crisis of capitalism has proved to be lengthy, intractable and met with increasingly desperate solutions. What would have been very straightforward questions with simple answers 30 years ago—how do we create full employment, where will the money come from for new hospitals, can we provide a good living standard for the old?—are now issues which bring into question the very future of capitalism. When the employers and government describe high unemployment as a natural disaster or hospital closures as a natural consequence of the market, those fighting on such issues have to be prepared to question the priorities of the system itself.

The working class movement will not be rebuilt on the old syndicalist notion of stronger unions alone, but will have politics—socialist politics—at its centre. Despite the relatively small number of socialists in workplaces today, their numbers are growing as a result of the series of economic and political crises internationally, and their influence on the industrial struggle is becoming greater. Socialists played a crucial role in Timex, in the UCH strike and in the resistance to pit closures. Unfortunately in none of these was their influence sufficiently strong to tip the balance in favour of victory rather than defeat. But the situation can change, both through the numerical growth of socialist organisation and through the influence it can exert on a much wider layer of militants.

The role of *Socialist Worker* is central to this. It can become the thread linking a network of militants far beyond the Socialist Workers Party, arguing for solidarity, rejecting the divisions inside the working class movement of race and sex, carrying an alternative strategy to that put forward by those at the top of the movement. It can therefore be the key to rebuilding strong rank and file organisation.

The early 1990s have seen the working class movement leave the worst years of the downturn. The government no longer dares to use a strategy such as the Ridley Plan which led to the defeat of one powerful group of workers after another. The employers do not at present have the confidence to organise a union busting operation like that organised by Rupert Murdoch at Wapping. The working class movement is poised on the brink of volatile struggles, the outcome of which is by no means certain or foreseeable. Either the workers' movement scores some decisive victories or eventually it can be once more defeated, with predictable consequences. Although there is a large politicised minority inside the working class movement, it lacks confidence and political direction. Socialist organisation and publications can help to provide that direction.

The period ahead will be stormy. The British ruling class is determined to force down the living standards of British workers at the same time as raising productivity. The 'social wage' will be further cut back. A deeply unpopular government will attempt to scapegoat various sections of society—from immigrants to New Age travellers. But discontent is certain to continue—taxation is set to rise, further cutting into already eroded real wages, and a further year of public sector pay freeze is under way.

At the same time, the battering the working class has taken under Thatcher and Major has left it fairly intact. Union membership remains high, at over 40 percent of employed workers.[114] The attitude of British workers is still very strongly in favour of state provision in areas such as health and welfare.[115] The lack of big industrial struggles in the past three years has a great deal to do with the caution of both the employers and the leaders of the working class movement. The signs are that the contradictions of British capitalism will lead that to change.

Notes

1   S Heffer, 'The Beginning of the End', *Spectator*, 16 October 1993.
2   See 'Pollwatch', *New Statesman and Society*, 3 September 1993.
3   Interview with John Redwood, *Independent*, 9 September 1993.
4   *High Hopes, Poor Strategies: Can Industry Plan for Growth?* (Pera International, London) p4.
5   Central Statistical Office figures, *Independent*, 15 September 1993.

6   Central Statistical Office figures, *Financial Times*, 22 September 1993.
7   *Financial Times*, 12 August 1993.
8   'Recovery slow but steady' (sic) by Robert Chote, *Independent*, 23 October 1993.
9   *Financial Times*, 16 August 1993.
10   *Economist*, 7 August 1993, p99.
11   See D Beecham, 'No Exit Ahead', in *Socialist Review*, June 1993.
12   A CBI survey published at the end of October showed manufacturing orders and output flat, export orders falling and industrial jobs going. Slow or no growth in continental Europe was held to be a major factor in this gloomy picture. See *Financial Times*, 27 October 1993.
13   Economics notebook by P Norman, *Financial Times*, 8 March 1993.
14   Ibid.
15   E Balls, 'Lurking Threat of First World Debt Crisis', *Financial Times*, 27 September 1993.
16   *Financial Times*, 13 August 1993.
17   See E Balls, *Financial Times*, 6 September 1993.
18   See B Clement, 'Anger Over Clarke Ultimatum', *Independent*, 15 September 1993.
19   Speech by Lord Lawson (formerly Nigel Lawson) to the British Association for the Advancement of Science (sic!), reported in *Financial Times*, 1 September 1993.
20   Gallup report by A King, *Daily Telegraph*, 6 August 1993.
21   See *Socialist Worker*, 23 February 1991, for reports of Tory disarray over the poll tax, and for reports of Labour councils attacking non-payers.
22   See *Socialist Worker*, 27 April 1991.
23   See *Socialist Worker*, 19 January 1991, 9 February 1991, 23 February 1991.
24   See *Socialist Worker*, 1 June 1991.
25   A Billen, 'Tory Party Blues', *Observer Magazine*, 26 September 1993.
26   Quoted in L German, 'The Crisis of British Politics', *Socialist Review* 168, October 1993.
27   S Heffer, 'The Beginning of the End', *Spectator*, 16 October 1993.
28   See L German, 'The Last Days of Thatcher?' in *International Socialism* 48, Autumn 1990, pp15-19, for both the unpopularity caused by attacks on public spending and the inability of the government to really cut substantially the proportion of national wealth which went into spending.
29   C Huhne, 'Tory Choice that Hurts the Poorest', *Independent on Sunday* (Business Section) 4 July 1993.
30   *Financial Times*, 13 August 1993.
31   E Balls, 'Missing the Unemployment-Deregulation Link', *Financial Times*, 6 September 1993.
32   Institute for Public Policy Research, *The Justice Gap* (London, 1993) p21.
33   Ibid, p29.
34   Ibid, p24.
35   *Social Trends*, (HMSO, London, 1992) p148.
36   C Huhne, op cit.
37   *The Justice Gap*, p44.
38   Ibid.
39   See *Households Below Average Income* (HMSO, London, 1993).
40   *The Justice Gap*, p47.
41   Ibid.
42   See *Independent*, 19 July 1993.
43   *Family Expenditure Survey*, quoted in *Observer*, 5 September 1993.
44   Ibid.
45   *Independent*, 8 September 1993.

46   H Young, *One of Us* (final edition, London, 1991) pp501-502.
47   Central Statistic Office figures, *Financial Times*, 22 September 1993.
48   *New Earnings Survey* 1993, Part A (HMSO, London).
49   Quoted in *Financial Times*, 16 August 1993.
50   *Incomes Data Services Report* 647, August 1993.
51   *New Earnings Survey* 1993, op cit.
52   C Huhne, 'Public Pay Policy is not Productive', *Independent on Sunday* (Business Section) 19 September 1993.
53   Interviewed in *Financial Times*, 26, 27 June 1993.
54   *New Earnings Survey*, op cit.
55   Bacon and Woodrow survey quoted in *Financial Times*, 11 October 1993.
56   *Social Trends* (HMSO, London, 1993) p90.
57   H Sutherland, 'Poorest could be hardest hit', *Independent*, 17 March 1993.
58   *Social Trends* (HMSO, London, 1992) p153.
59   Ibid, p154.
60   E Tucker, 'Debt tightens its grip and threatens to hit recovery', *Financial Times*, 29 July 1993.
61   *Financial Times*, 9 July 1993.
62   In response to the question, 'Why do you think there are people who live in need?' a Eurobarometer survey in 1976 showed the following responses: because they have been unlucky 10 percent, because of laziness or lack of willpower 43 percent, because of injustice in our society 16 percent, and it's an inevitable part of modern life 17 percent. A study in 1983 put the responses at 13 percent, 22 percent, 32 percent and 25 percent respectively, while a 1986 study showed 11 percent, 19 percent, 25 percent and 37 percent. There was a marked increase in those who blamed it on injustice or an inevitable part of modern life, while there was an even steeper fall in those who blamed the individuals concerned. See *British Social Attitudes* (Aldershot, 1987), p10.
63   'Redundancy fear survives upturn', *Financial Times*, 31 August 1993.
64   ICM poll, *Guardian*, 17 September 1993.
65   ICM poll, *Guardian*, 18 September 1993.
66   *Observer* and Cassell poll, *Observer*, 5 September 1993.
67   'Public services rapped', *Financial Times*, 26 August 1993.
68   'Social and Economic Trends for Local Government' survey, quoted in UNISON magazine, London, October 1993..
69   *Socialist Worker*, 13 October 1990.
70   *Socialist Worker*, 27 October 1990.
71   *Socialist Worker*, 17 November 1990.
72   *Socialist Worker*, 27 October 1990.
73   The most notorious example at the time was at Toleman's in Essex. See *Socialist Worker*, 27 October 1990.
74   *Socialist Worker*, 10 November 1990.
75   *Socialist Worker*, 12 January 1991.
76   *Socialist Worker*, 26 January 1991.
77   See *Socialist Worker*, 6 April 1991 and 13 April 1991.
78   *Socialist Worker*, 4 May 1991.
79   *Socialist Worker*, 11 May 1991 and 18 May 1991.
80   *Socialist Worker*, 18 May 1991.
81   *Socialist Worker*, 1 June 1991 and 25 May 1991.
82   *Socialist Worker*, 20 July 1991.
83   *Socialist Worker*, 22 June 1991.
84   *Socialist Worker*, 12 October 1991.
85   *Socialist Worker*, 9 November 1991.
86   *Socialist Worker*, 12 October 1991.

87   *Socialist Worker,* 22 February 1992 and 7 March 1992.
88   *Socialist Worker,* 14 March 1992 and 28 March 1992.
89   *Socialist Worker,* 20 June 1992.
90   For a much more detailed (though still incomplete) list of who came from where see C Kimber, 'On the Move', in *Socialist Review,* November 1992.
91   See *Socialist Worker,* 24 October, 31 October and 7 November 1992.
92   *Socialist Worker,* 28 November 1992.
93   See 'Five Tories defy whip in coal vote', *Financial Times,* 28 October 1993.
94   *Social Trends* (HMSO, London, 1992) p59, and see Appendix, pt 4, p191.
95   *Socialist Worker,* 4 July 1992.
96   *Socialist Worker,* 21 August 1993.
97   G Elliott, *Labourism and the English Genius* (London, 1993) pp161-162.
98   Pollwatch, *New Statesman,* 3 September 1993.
99   Survey reported in *Guardian,* 25 September 1993.
100   Ibid.
101   Indicative of this is the change in composition of the constituency section of Labour's NEC, once the bastion of the left, now not even including Tony Benn, and electing such right wingers as Gordon Brown and Tony Blair (although interestingly at the 1993 Labour conference both received lower votes than in 1992).
102   I Aitken, 'Brown's Thatcherite gobbledegook', *New Statesman,* 3 September 1993.
103   Quoted in *Observer,* 12 September 1993.
104   'Local party basing success on traditional brand of socialism', *Guardian,* 25 September 1993.
105   See 'Conference Notebook' by P Stephens, *Financial Times,* 30 September 1993.
106   Ibid.
107   John Monks interviewed in *Independent on Sunday,* 5 September 1993.
108   Quoted in *Financial Times,* 6 October 1993.
109   Quoted in *Financial Times,* 18 September 1993.
110   Survey carried out by the Centre for Economic Performance at the London School of Economics, quoted in *Financial Times,* 31 August 1993.
111   Reported by *Socialist Worker* journalist Mike Simons and SWP miners about a meeting in Armthorpe, Yorkshire, in November 1992 when Scargill rounded on the left.
112   T Cliff, 'The Balance of Class Forces', *International Socialism* 6, Autumn 1979, p45.
113   Ibid, p45.
114   See 'Notes of the Month', *Socialist Review,* October 1993. Also see *Social Trends* (HMSO, London, 1993) pp158-159.
115   Britain ranked with Italy as top of several countries (the others were the US, Australia, West Germany and Austria) for believing that government should provide health care, and decent living standards for the old and unemployed, and reduce income differences between rich and poor. See *British Social Attitudes,* special international report (Aldershot, 1989) p41.

The 'politically correct' controversy

JOHN MOLYNEUX

The debate over Political Correctness has been going on in the United States for several years and it is to some extent already an issue in Britain. The tabloids are handling the question in their usual style. More 'serious' journalists such as Simon Hoggart and Melanie Phillips have also jumped on the anti-PC bandwagon. But what is PC? Despite the capital letters it is not an organisation, a campaign or even a movement. There are no recognised PC leaders, no official or even unofficial PC programme or manifesto. Nor is it even possible to identify key theoretical texts which exemplify the PC outlook. At most, perhaps, it could be described as a trend, a cultural phenomenon, a series of attitudes and practices which are an effect or residue of certain aspects of the movements for black, female and gay liberation. Indeed PC did not even name itself. The term 'politically correct' appears to have originated within the left. Paul Berman tells us that:

> 'Politically Correct' was originally a phrase on the Leninist left to denote someone who steadfastly toed the party line. Then it evolved into 'PC', an ironic phrase among wised up leftists to denote someone whose line-toeing fervour was too much to bear. Only in connection with the PC debate itself did the phrase get picked up by people who had no fidelity to radicalism at all, but who relished the nasty syllables for their twist of irony.[1]

For this reason the analysis of PC is best approached by starting with its opponents on the right whose attacks have constructed it as a bogey.

In retrospect it is clear that an opening shot in the anti-PC campaign was fired by the right wing University of Chicago philosopher Allan Bloom with his 1987 book *The Closing of the American Mind*. This rather bizarre work, which denounced not only the student revolt of the 1960s and its consequences but also rock music, was dedicated to the proposition that universities and especially American universities were the 'home of reason' and the disinterested pursuit of truth until undermined by radical 'relativists'. Such an eccentric production contained too many hostages to fortune to launch a crusade but nonetheless met with extraordinary success—more than six months at the top of the *New York Times* best seller list.

> *Bloom demonstrated to publishers and potential authors one thesis beyond doubt: it is possible to write an alarmist book about the state of higher education with a long winded title and make a great deal of money.*[2]

Bloom was soon followed by educational journalist Roger Kimball's *Tenured Radicals: How Politics has Corrupted Our Higher Education* and Dinesh D'Souza's *Illiberal Education: the Politics of Race and Sex on Campus* which rapidly became 'the bible of the anti-PC campaign'[3]. D'Souza's work achieved this status partly thanks to the author's political acuity. For the purposes of his attack on PC he adopted a political standpoint substantially to the left of his real position. D'Souza was a hard right winger, a policy adviser in the Reagan White House and biographer of Jerry Falwell, yet in *Illiberal Education* he presents himself as a supporter of Martin Luther King, an anti-racist and a sympathiser with the plight of black students. To his political godfathers 'liberal' was the 'L' word with which they baited their Democratic opponents, but D'Souza claims to write in defence of liberal education. Accordingly he writes in a tone of sweet reasonableness, merely raising issues for debate and making 'modest proposals'[4]. This doesn't change in any way the profoundly right wing character of the book but it does make it possible to win plaudits from the likes of Eugene Genovese.[5]

Part stimulating, part swimming in the wake of the relatively heavyweight tones of Messrs Bloom, Kimball and D'Souza, came innumerable articles in *Newsweek*, the *New York Times*, the *New York Review Of Books*, the *New Republic*, the *Village Voice*, the *Wall Street Journal* and almost every other US paper, magazine or journal of note. Before long even the indolent George Bush had noticed that something was up and decided that it would aid his chances of re-election to join the onslaught. Addressing students at the University of Michigan in May 1991 he declared, 'Political extremists roam the land, abusing the privilege of free speech, setting citizens against one another on the basis of their class or race.'[6] With Bush in the field, supported by other leading

Republicans such as former education secretary William Bennett and National Endowment for the Humanities chair Lynne Cheney (wife of defence secretary, Dick Cheney) the attack on PC could only intensify.

In a short article such as this it is obviously impossible to document or even summarise all the charges and arguments produced by this conservative campaign, but the essence of their case can be summed up fairly easily. It is that America's universities have been, or are in the process of being, taken over by a new alliance of radical faculty members (lecturers) and student activists who are destroying the hallowed traditions of American academia and higher education through their obsession with the politics of race and sex. The key weapons of the radicals are said to be affirmative action, ie positive efforts to recruit hitherto under-represented ethnic minority students (basically blacks and Hispanics) which is lowering academic standards, curriculum revision designed to attack the canon of Western civilisation and culture, and language codes prohibiting racial and sexual abuse which contravene the right to free speech. The effect of this leftist subversion is to transform the universities into citadels of totalitarian intolerance in which racial antagonisms are increased, honest academic inquiry inhibited and 'ordinary' students and 'moderate' or traditional staff members walk in fear of constant repression and harassment by PC fanatics.

Before dealing in detail with these specific issues, some of which present quite knotty problems, some general observations on the nature of the anti-PC campaign are in order. First it should be noted that in America the debate has focused primarily on the narrow terrain of the university, with only limited overspill into other areas (the schools, arts, etc). In Britain, a point I shall return to later, the key terrain for the PC battle seems likely to be elsewhere, for example the social services.

Second, the issue which in Britain seems most to have caught people's attention, namely euphemistic language reform (calling short people 'vertically challenged' etc) has only been one small aspect of the debate and not the one which has generated most heat. Far more important have been the fights over affirmative action and the literary heritage.

Third, while the anti-PC campaign was clearly launched by and has been dominated by right wing forces, in its latter stages it attracted at least qualified support from some surprising sources. I have already mentioned the erstwhile Marxist historian Eugene Genovese but others from the left, or at least left of centre, who have weighed in on the anti-PC side include Nat Hentoff of the *Village Voice*[7], veteran social democrat Irving Howe[8] and perhaps most surprising of all Edward Said, who as the author of *Orientalism* and *Culture and Imperialism* many would have identified as himself a PCer[9]. Paul Berman notes 'the way that certain liberals and old-school leftists joined the neo-conservatives in making several of the arguments as something new and perhaps quite significant, since previous debates tended to observe a chaste division of left and right'[10].

At this point it is necessary to mention the intervention of Robert Hughes, author of the best selling history of modern art *The Shock of the New* and the art critic of *Time* magazine. In 1993 Hughes published *Culture of Complaint—The Fraying of America*, which in a number of ways is a quite distinctive contribution to the debate. Firstly Hughes broadens the focus from the university to American culture as a whole which he sees as having become an 'infantilized culture of complaint', a 'broken polity' polarised between the 'twin fetishes of victimhood and redemption'[11]. Secondly, unlike D'Souza and Co, he does not concentrate his attack exclusively on the left. Instead from a position of robust 'commonsense' liberalism he treats the politically correct of the left and the 'patriotically correct' of the right (the likes of Pat Robertson, Pat Buchanan and Jessie Helms who dominated the pre-election Republican Convention of 1992) as mirror images of each other, twin descendants of America's witch hunting puritan past; and lambasts both with equal fervour. Thirdly, and this is also in contrast to most of the literature on the subject, Hughes writes with such gusto and panache that it is hard not to be beguiled by him even when one is in sharp political disagreement with a number of his arguments[12]. Nevertheless, despite these distinctions, it was inevitable, given the context and timing of its production, that *Culture of Complaint* would be received and taken up primarily as a blow against PC.

This then is the anti-PC line up: a formidable array comprising almost all strands of the American media stretching politically from the far right to the liberal left.

Bush's election defeat in 1992 took some of the wind out of the anti-PCers' sails. Bush's attempt to win re-election on the back of conservative cultural themes like 'family values' failed. But the potency of the issues on which the anti-PC campaign focused remains. In June 1993 President Bill Clinton withdrew his nomination of a liberal Black civil rights enforcement appointee following a conservative campaign that labelled her a 'quota queen'. And campus anti-feminists have recently taken to labelling women who speak out against date rape as 'sexually correct'.

The socialist response

A socialist response to the anti-PC campaign has to both analyse the debate as a whole, examining the social forces and politics involved on both sides, and also respond to a number of specific issues raised by the debate which present themselves as concrete practical questions in workplaces, colleges and elsewhere quite independently of our choosing. At the general level the most striking feature of the anti-PC campaign is the disproportion between its rhetoric and the enemy which it is attacking. Irving Kristol claimed in the *Wall Street Journal* that 'multiculturalism is as much a "war against the West" as Nazism and Stalinism ever were'[13]. George Will argued that the war against the politicisation of higher education was more important than the war against Iraq[14], while one of the most common charges against PC has been that it is a new McCarthyism. Thus December 1990 *Newsweek* headlined its key PC article 'Is this the New Enlightenment or the New McCarthyism?' only to be echoed a few months later by Eugene Genovese: 'I fear that our conservative colleagues are today facing a new McCarthyism in some ways more effective and vicious than the old.'[15]

There is a bitter irony in the accusation of McCarthyism for it is clearly the anti-PC crusaders of the right who are the spiritual heirs of the junior senator from Wisconsin, but it is also an absurd overestimation of the PC forces. It should be remembered that McCarthyism at its height had the power to arraign before Congress, fire, blacklist, deport, drive into exile and imprison thousands of supposed Communists and leftists from all walks of life including Hollywood, teaching, and academia itself, whereas not a single academic has been sacked as a result of PC activity. The real McCarthyism was able to persecute not just Paul Robeson, Bertolt Brecht and Arthur Miller but a figure with the standing of Charlie Chaplin. If PC had comparable power Arnold Schwarzenegger would be on the plane back to Austria and Clint Eastwood out of a job, not raking in Oscars.

Even the more soberly expressed claim of D'Souza and Kimball that PC culture now dominates America's universities is plainly false. Such wild exaggeration is built into the structure of D'Souza's book, for his method is to select typical PC offences, illustrate them with 'case studies' from particular colleges—hence 'admission policy at Berkeley', 'multiculturalism at Stanford' and so on—and pass the results off as a representative survey of American higher education. It is as if someone were to present a picture of crime in Britain based on case studies of the Yorkshire Ripper, Dennis Nielson and the Moors Murderers.

Reading Kimball and D'Souza one has repeatedly to pinch oneself to remember the elementary fact that America's universities (like British and other universities) are businesses in their own right and tied by a thousand threads to the giant corporations and the state including, of course, the military. Radical feminists, black militants, left wing socialists, neo-Marxists and the like do not run America's universities and never will this side of a revolution. In so far as such people exist in the colleges they are a minority influence concentrated in junior positions. The Higher Education Research Institute 1989-90 Survey of 35,000 faculty members of 392 US colleges and universities showed that 40 percent identified themselves as 'moderates', 37 percent as 'liberals', 18 percent as 'conservatives' and only 5 percent as 'far left'.[16]

Even Robert Hughes, though dissociating himself from Genovese's McCarthyism charge[17] and other extravagant claims, is still prone to this exaggeration. It is a central weakness of *Culture of Complaint* that the book is premised on equating the two PCs, politically and patriotically correct, both morally and in terms of their significance. To imagine that Leonard Jeffries, Paula Rothenburg or the Black Faculty Caucus at the University of Texas[18] are the equal of Jerry Falwell, Pat Buchanan or William Bennett (not to speak of Bush) in terms of status and power in American society is absurd. The error derives from Hughes' over-concentration on the cultural sphere to the exclusion of the economic. As a result he fails to see that 'the fraying of America' which he detects is far more the product of the ongoing crisis of US capitalism than of particular statements and attitudes of journalists, academics and politicians. Enthusiasm for his polemic also leads Hughes into rhetorical lapses of his own. When deploring pro-choice disruption of a *Village Voice* sponsored debate on abortion he immediately reaches for the imagery of fascism, 'the jackboot and the gag...Brownshirt ranting'.[19]

Exaggeration and scaremongering however are familiar features of right wing thinking and propaganda. Think of McCarthy himself with his delusions of Communist influence in the US army or the perennial racist inflation of immigration figures and those fears that the 'great' British culture is about to be 'swamped', or all that hysteria about extreme influence in the Labour Party. No doubt the paranoia is partly genuine, reflecting a nagging suspicion in conservative minds that one day the Earth may open up beneath their feet and swallow them up; no doubt there is an element of sincere shock that hallowed traditions should be challenged at all, but exaggerating the forces of the left (especially when the left is relatively weak) also has the strategic function of disguising the real purposes of a campaign and winning 'moderate' support for far right wing views. Demonising Saddam Hussein as the new Hitler helped sell a war on the Iraqi people for control of oil. McCarthy's anti-Communist witch hunt masked an attack on trade unionism and New Deal liberalism. The assault on *Militant* in the Labour Party was used to defeat Bennism and tame the soft left.

The next question socialists have to ask therefore is, what is the real target of the anti-PC campaign? The answer is pretty plain: it is what remains of the gains of the movements of the 1960s and early 1970s. The attack on PC is part of the much wider ruling class project to 'roll back the 1960s' which has included the attack on unions, the attack on welfare, the war on drugs with its criminalisation of the inner cities and overcoming the Vietnam syndrome by serial invasions of Grenada, Panama, Iraq and Somalia.

The great radical movements of the 1960s (and to be accurate, the early 1970s)—the black movement, the student revolt and the anti-war movement—fell apart in the mid-1970s, part crushed, part exhausted and part incorporated, but they left a legacy. Racism remained, of course, but the laws, the culture and the consciousness of mainstream America with regard to race were significantly changed. So too was the consciousness of black Americans—Malcolm X was killed but not forgotten. There was also the emergence of a substantial black middle class, as both price and condition of the defeat of black revolution. The women's movement and to a lesser extent the lesbian and gay movement had similar effects.

The universities were also changed. Mass student activism subsided but a generation of teachers who had lived through the 1960s, even if they themselves had not been activists or had moved to the right, could not simply return to the smug conservatism and stifling conformity of the 1950s. In the humanities and social sciences the old certainties of art for art's sake, cold war politics and functionalist sociology were no longer good enough even for 'moderates' and liberals. At the same time the combination of social change and affirmative action meant that the student population ceased to be virtually all white, which itself inevitably put new demands on the curriculum. For the right wing the campaign against PC is the intellectual equivalent of the invasions of Grenada and Panama. They see it as an opportunity to start turning the clock back to the imagined golden age of elitist higher education unsullied by the politics of race and sex.[20]

It is therefore clear that in the PC war socialists must in general side with the left and counter-attack against the right. In that sense we must defend PC. But what kind of defence should this be? One possibility is to take advantage of the distortions and exaggeration in the anti-PC campaign to enter a plea of not guilty, ie to argue that it is all a case of right wing hype and that nothing particularly radical or controversial is happening. This option is likely to be attractive to academics and professionals who, while well meaning and progressive, are not political activists and lack a worked out political perspective.[21]

Another possibility is aggressive support for PC and all its works: an approach which sees the PC fight as the latest frontline in the struggle against racism, sexism and homophobia and tends to assume that all opposition and criticism is simply a manifestation of covert bigotry flushed out by PC's iconoclastic attack on the assumptions of white Western civilisation.[22] This response is perhaps most likely to be adopted by militant black nationalists and radical feminists.

However, for Marxists neither of these options is satisfactory. In the first place it is clear that the PC phenomenon does exist, if only on a limited scale and only as kind of cultural mood, so simple denial will not do. It is also a fact that some of the things done in the name of PC are, to put it charitably, simply silly. Consider the testimony of Edward Said. Said was presenting a paper based on aspects of his book *Culture and Imperialism* to an advanced historical studies seminar. Its theme was 'the emergence of a global consciousness in Western knowledge at the end of the 19th century', which he argued, coincides with a fully global imperial perspective:

> *The first question after my brief resume was from a professor of history, a black woman of some eminence who had recently come to the university, but whose work was unfamiliar to me. She announced in advance that her question was to be hostile, 'a very hostile one in fact'. She then said something like the following: 'For the first 13 pages of your paper you talked about white European males, thereafter, on page 14 you mention some names of non-Europeans. How could you do such a thing?' I remonstrated somewhat. After all, I said, I was discussing European imperialism, which would not have been likely to include in its discourse the work of African-American women. I pointed out that in the book I say quite a bit about the response to imperialism all over the world...[including] such writers as...CLR James. To this my critic replied with a stupefying confidence that my answer was not satisfactory since CLR James was dead![23]*

That an academic of Said's standing and anti-Eurocentric credentials should be criticised *in this way* (as opposed to a number of other ways in which he could quite reasonably be criticised) and that he should be driven by PC zealots to public protest is a sign both that something is up and that something is wrong.

Of course socialists support and identify with all struggles against oppression and bigotry, and some PC activity, or activity which is attacked as PC, comes under this heading. But it is also possible for well intentioned (as well as not so well intentioned) anti-racists and anti-sexists to adopt strategies, tactics and positions that are ineffective or even counter-productive and when this happens socialists have a duty to criticise—without however lining up with the right.

The basic problem with PC derives ultimately from its social location. Essentially it is a middle class phenomenon, which is not to say that PC issues cannot arise within the working class movement, but its social roots lie in those sections of the left and of the black, women's and gay movements which have attained positions of relative comfort and authority within bourgeois society. Moreover at its heart PC is an attempt to use those positions of authority to impose anti-racism, anti-sexism and so on from above. In America, as we have seen, PC culture is concentrated in the universities (and in some of the most elite campuses), but it is not in the main associated with mass student revolt against the government or the university authorities, rather it is primarily an attempt to pressurise the authorities and even enlist them as allies. Hence its rather prim and proper character. It is impossible to imagine a genuine mass movement from below—a revolutionary upsurge of the working class or even an uprising of the mass of the oppressed like that in Los Angeles—being 'politically correct'. For it is in the nature of such a movement that it draws into the struggle the previously backward, unorganised and uneducated who come with many of their old prejudices, habits of thought and speech intact.

All too often PC makes a mistake paralleling the errors of its opponents: the inflation of the importance of the sphere of education and culture and the neglect of the sphere of material conditions and relations of production. Barbara Ehrenreich sums it up when she writes, 'I've noticed students that I would characterise as PC who get very worked up about imagined or real verbal slights, but you don't see them running en masse to support campus workers when they're organising or striking'.[24] Typically PC is characterised by a cultural idealism and moralism which is the besetting sin of intellectuals cut off from the working class and the mass movement.

PC is also a good deal less radical than its proponents imagine, firmly reformist rather than revolutionary. In the PC pantheon of 'race, gender and class' class has always come a very poor third,[25] but the pursuit of race and gender equality detached from the struggle of the working class inevitable proceeds in a reformist direction more or less regardless of rhetoric or subjective intentions. This is because objectively neither blacks on their own, nor women, nor lesbians and gays have the material power to overthrow American capitalism and its power structure; consequently their focus inevitably shifts to the demand for inclusion within the existing capitalist hierarchy. Nor is PC by any means the most radical form of reformism. Despite all the talk of the 'rights' and 'empowerment' the main tactic of PC is to appeal to the consciences of 'the oppressors' on the basis of moral guilt. Hence the PC cult of victim status so excoriated by D'Souza and Hughes.[26] Unfortunately it is far easier to guilt trip an idealist student or a liberal intellectual than the US ruling class. Guilt is also a very poor basis for fighting racism and other reactionary ideas in the working class. The mass of white workers will be won to anti-racism and unity with black workers through an understanding of their common class interest, not through guilt over the legacy of slavery (for which they were not responsible in the first place).

Therefore, while Marxists and socialists must start from a position of exposing the anti-PC witch hunters and defending PC against the right, the defence must be a highly critical one. Some idea of the exact combination of support and criticism required is best provided in an examination of a number of concrete issues.

Affirmative action

Dinesh D'Souza places the issue of affirmative action (ie: positive discrimination in the recruitment of black and Hispanic students) at the centre of his attack on PC. Affirmative action was, as we have noted, one of the 'gains' of the 1960s—indeed in material terms it was, along with the abolition of Jim Crow in the south, one of the most important gains. It was always, however, an ambiguous advance. On the one hand it was a concession—rung from the ruling class by the combined weight of the Civil Rights Movement, black power and inner city insurrections from Watts to Detroit. On the other hand it was a key element in the ruling class strategy to defeat and divide the black movement through the deliberate creation of a substantial black middle class—a strategy that was at least partially successful. Despite this ambiguity the central argument in favour of affirmative action, namely that a degree of positive discrimination is essential if blacks are to overcome the racism built into American education and American society for so long, is one that both socialists and the wider US left have generally supported.

From its inception affirmative action was subject to right wing resistance and counter-attack on the grounds that it constituted 'reverse discrimination' and an infringement on the individual rights of whites. One thing that seems to unite racists and oppressors across the world from the white South Africans to Ulster Unionists is their extreme sensitivity to the slightest hint that they may find themselves in the position of underdog. To those of like mind in America affirmative action was a red rag to a bull.

In 1977 the case of Bakke v The University of California at Davis came before the Supreme Court. Alan Bakke had failed to gain admission to medical school at Davis at a time when the school reserved 16 of its 100 places for 'disadvantaged' students. Claiming that his academic record was superior to some of the 16 'minority' students Bakke maintained he had been discriminated against. In 1978 the Supreme Court by a five to four majority found in favour of Bakke, but it was to some extent an equivocal decision. On the one hand the court ruled that the use of an 'explicit racial classification' where no formal discriminatory behaviour had been demonstrated was unconstitutional. On the other hand, it also found again by five to four, that affirmative action which made race 'simply one element' in the admission process was permissible 'since universities had a legitimate interest in seeking diversity in their student populations'.[27] In 1990 the Bush administration issued regulations restricting the ability of colleges to award financial aid to minority students. And a civil rights bill intended to reverse some of the Supreme Court's most far-reaching attacks on affirmative action, passed by the Democratic led Congress in 1992, explicitly outlawed the use of quotas for affirmative action. Thus affirmative action has continued in American universities but under increasing pressure and on a diminishing scale, with the result that, whereas in the 1960s and 1970s the number of blacks attending college expanded enormously,[28] in the 1980s the proportions of black high school graduates going to higher education started to fall.[29]

It was against this background of affirmative action in retreat that D'Souza launched his offensive. He is careful not to mount his challenge directly in the name of white majority, but begins by taking up cudgels on behalf of Asian-American (ie Japanese, Korean, Chinese) students and then, apparently, on behalf of black and Hispanic students themselves. First he presents individual case studies and statistics to show that Berkeley's admission policy, which is striving for proportional representation of ethnic minorities, results in Asian students with good grades having less chance of admission than similar black students, due to the fact that Asians over-achieve at high school while blacks under-achieve. Then he moves on to argue that this policy damages black students themselves as the feeling that they are only there because of affirmative action undermines their self esteem, and their inability to compete with better prepared white and Asian students leads to a high drop out rate. Finally he suggests that it is affirmative action which is responsible for increased racial tension, separatism and even for the wave of outright racial incidents that swept American campuses in the late 1980s:

> *Separatist black and Hispanic groups became a haven from the anxieties that spring from the sharp differences in academic preparations among various racial groups. Indeed separatism can serve as a form of group therapy, in which affirmative action beneficiaries persuade themselves that their difficulties on campus are predominately, if not exclusively, the consequence of rampant bigotry...*
>
> *Many white and Asian students reciprocate in kind, because they are offended by what they see as university-sponsored discrimination against them...some respond with barely suppressed exasperation whenever they see black and Hispanic students make the slightest mistake, or congregate together on any occasion.*[30]

Let us take the last argument first. D'Souza's language is cautious but essentially what he says is that white racist activity like assaults on black students by a white mob at Massachusetts or arson of a black fraternity house at the University of Mississippi,[31] are the result, almost the 'inevitable' and 'excusable' result, of affirmative action. The structure of this argument should be familiar. It is the same logic which 'explains' and partly justifies racist violence in Germany or Britain by the *presence* of too many immigrants who are supposed to be taking over 'our' houses, 'our' jobs and so on. It is based on the assumption that if the black presence were reduced numerically the racist resentment would fade. The falsity of this assumption is demonstrated not only by the history of immigration and immigration control, but also by the history of American universities themselves which for centuries remained almost exclusively white without any disappearance of racism.[32] Rather it is the campaigners against affirmative action, like D'Souza himself, and a number of other senior Republicans, who are encouraging such racism.

To D'Souza's arguments about unfairness to Asian students and damage to black and Hispanic students' self esteem and so on socialists have a simple answer—an egalitarian system of higher education open to all. Of course it would be objected that such a solution is not realistic. But we should be clear about *why* it is 'unrealistic'. It is not that American society couldn't afford it. It is that the American ruling class wouldn't grant it. It is that even if higher education were made open to all it would not be egalitarian (the ruling class would ensure that some colleges were more privileged than others) because America is a competitive, class divided society in which the primary function of education is not the enlightenment and development of the population as a whole but the selection and training of the bourgeoisie and the middle class. But then revolutionary socialists are revolutionary not because they prefer revolution to reform but because the contradictions and evils of capitalist society cannot be removed solely by means of reform.

In the absence of an egalitarian system socialists must continue their support for affirmative action. The alternative is to side with the racists and the right and see the black and Hispanic student presence dwindle to a tiny minority of the offspring of the upper reaches of the already established black and Hispanic middle class. Socialists must combine this with support for every measure that improves the general education and wider socio-economic position of blacks, Hispanics and other oppressed groups whose acute educational difficulties are the cumulative result of capitalist slavery, capitalist imperialism and capitalist racism.

At the same time socialists should have no illusions as to what affirmative action can achieve. The most it can do is to provide some opportunities for some students who would not otherwise have had them. It cannot end racism nor create genuine equality in society as a whole or even within higher education. It cannot even manage to be 'completely' fair even in its own terms. An unequal, racist, sexist society cannot be put right by means of educational social engineering. Education both reflects and shapes society. Socialists fight for it to shape society in an egalitarian direction but must recognise the material fact that the element of reflection inevitably outweighs the element of shaping. More fundamental change can be achieved only by a mass movement in which students, teachers and professors can play a role but which must be led by the working class.

Speech codes

The question of speech codes has been one of the most controversial issues in the PC debate. Many universities responded to the outbursts of racism and bigotry in the late 1980s by establishing codes making the use of abusive and offensive language pertaining to race, gender, and sexual orientation—perhaps best described as 'hate speech'—into a disciplinary offence. A coalition of the right, much of the media, and liberals, including the influential American Civil Liberties Union, have attacked speech codes as violations of the principle of free speech, a principle which in America has the special status of being enshrined in the First Amendment to the constitution.

Many of those currently invoking the First Amendment against university speech codes can easily be exposed as the most obvious hypocrites: people who rush to the defence of the most vile racism, while demanding censorship of anti-religious, left wing or sexually explicit language that they find offensive. A good example is Republican Henry Hyde who sponsored legislation in Congress to outlaw speech codes but who has also 'co-sponsored a constitutional amendment to ban flag burning, endorsed the Helms amendment to deny federal funding for "homoerotic" art and supports the regulation barring abortion counselling in federal funded health clinics'.[33] Such people are the political or intellectual equivalent of police who defend the right of Nazis to march through black or immigrant areas on the grounds of 'democracy' while systematically persecuting those same black people and attacking left wing or anti-racist demonstrations.

However, not all those in the anti speech codes campaign fall into this category. Some like Nat Hentoff, who has spent 'three years of reporting on anti free speech tendencies in higher education'[34] for the *Village Voice*, the *Washington Post* and the *New Yorker*, appear to be genuine liberals who actually believe in freedom of speech as an absolute principle. Therefore there is an argument that has to be taken on intellectually. Literary theorist Stanley Fish, in an article entitled 'There's No Such Thing as Free Speech and It's a Good Thing Too', cites the example of Milton:

> Not far from the end of his **Aeropagitica** and after having celebrated the virtues of toleration and unregulated publication in passages that find their way into every discussion of free speech and the First Amendment, John Milton catches himself up short, and says of course I didn't mean Catholics, them we exterminate. 'I mean not tolerated popery and open superstition,

*which as it extirpates all religions and civil supremacies, so itself should be
extirpated.'*[35]

Fish's point is well made. The fact is that no society has ever per-
mitted total freedom of speech without any restrictions whatsoever and it
is hard to see how it could. Certainly in contemporary America and
Britain and every other bourgeois democracy there are a multitude of
restraints on free speech. First there are legal limitations like the Official
Secrets Act, the libel and slander laws, laws against incitement to riot or
violence, blasphemy laws and so on. Even more important there are
institutional rules which curtail rights of free speech in innumerable situations. Imagine a soldier trying to exercise his freedom of speech to a
superior officer or child to a head teacher or even a student to a college
president. A large number of employers place restrictions on their
employees' freedom to speak about their work or to go to the press.
These restrictions are usually presented as matters of respect for
authority, or not bringing the company into dispute or just good manners,
but they remain restrictions on freedom of speech nonetheless. The
problem with almost all liberals is that they simply don't notice all these
violations of their 'absolute' principle, they just take them for granted.
So if a worker is sacked for telling the manager to fuck off, or a defen-
dant is sent down for contempt of court for calling a judge a geriatric git,
that is accepted as normal, but if a student or professor is disciplined for
using race or sex hate words, that becomes an issue of freedom of
speech.

A further difficulty for those who try to make the claims of free
speech inviolate is the impossibility of drawing an absolute dividing line
between words and deeds. Consider the example of blackmail. This is
generally accepted as being a crime, yet it may consist entirely of words.
'Pay me £1,000 or I will tell the papers your guilty secret.' Then there is
the cynical politician who deliberately incites racism. Is he or she any
less guilty than the thug who beats someone on the street? Racist, sexist
and homophobic epithets are on this borderline between speech and
action. There are many situations in which they are associated with violence and can lead to violence and in which they cause as much hurt or
offence as violence.

Taking all these considerations into account, it is clear that 'freedom
of speech' cannot legitimately be invoked to defeat or protect hate
speech. Moreover socialists, whose whole aim is to unite the working
class and fight all forms of oppression, have special reason to combat
these disgusting and divisive terms. Therefore, in general terms, attempts
to combat abusive language have to be defended. Once again, however,
it cannot be an uncritical defence. Speech codes have a number of
defects which socialists must not lose sight of. First there is the obvious

point that outlawing certain expressions does not in itself change attitudes or ideas. Thus there is the fact that speech codes are normally drawn up and imposed by university administrators, rather than emerging from below, and consequently are bureaucratically operated. This in itself is likely to compromise and alienate the codes in the eyes of students by associating them with the rest of university's authority structure and disciplinary procedures.

There is also the danger that politically sophisticated right wingers will dance rings round any speech code while non-political and unsophisticated students may fall foul of it. This is especially likely if it is mechanically and pedantically applied. Such cases are then likely to be seized on by the right and the media to discredit anti-racism and anti-sexism as a whole.

Finally there is the likelihood that speech codes will be used against the left rather than the bigots. It is easy to imagine situations where calling scabs scabs or Nazis Nazis would become disciplinary offences. Selfa and Maass give an example from Harvard where a white Southern student was allowed to hang a Confederate flag in her dormitory while a black woman was required to remove a 'No Racism' banner bearing a swastika, and cite the University of Michigan where the authorities did nothing when right wingers destroyed shanty towns built by anti-apartheid and Palestinian activists but disciplined student journalists who criticised Israel.

For all these reasons the best strategy for student activists is not to rely on speech codes but to concentrate on mobilising students for collective struggles against racism, sexism and homophobia. If this is done the social pressure of student opinion will be far more effective than codes in discouraging hate speech.

Language reform

It is through its attempts to promote language reform that PC, certainly in this country, has gained its greatest notoriety and been subject to the most ridicule (though as we noted earlier this has not been its most controversial aspect in America). Language reform is related to the attempt to outlaw hate speech but is also distinct from it. All the main terms of racist, sexist and homophobic abuse are well known parts of everyday speech and their insulting nature is commonly acknowledged. Also they all have perfectly straightforward non-offensive alternatives already in common use. Eliminating hate speech therefore involves little more than omitting certain deliberately derogatory and offensive expressions.

In contrast language reform involves discovering pejorative or oppressive meanings in words or expressions where none was previously acknowledged and attempting to replace them with new, often artificially created, words and expressions. At the same time even the strongest supporters of PC have not generally tried to make use of these neologisms a disciplinary matter (though doubtless there is an exception somewhere). Rather the attempt is to reform the language through example, moral pressure and sometimes administrative measures.

Language has of course always been a political issue and political struggles have always involved battles over language. In the Reformation the translation of the Bible into common language was a political question. The suppression of native languages by conquerors— a common practice ranging from the banning of Gaelic in the Highlands to the prohibition of Kurdish in Turkey—has always been a political question. Forms of address, sensitive indicators of social rank, have always been political. In *The Revolution Betrayed* Trotsky indicted the Stalinist bureaucrats for their habitual use of the second person singular with subordinates and workers. 'How can they fail to remember', he asks, 'that one of the most popular revolutionary slogans in Tsarist Russia was the demand for the abolition of the use of the second person singular by bosses in addressing their subordinates'.[36] Revolutions in thought have introduced new terms and concepts which are important to the new way of understanding the world but which at first may seem strange or obscure. It makes a difference whether we speak of the 'creation' or the 'evolution' of the species, whether we call modern society 'industrial' or 'capitalist', whether we demand a 'people's state' or a 'workers' state'. Revolutions in practice have always led to the renaming of cities and streets, to calling people citizen or comrade instead of sir or master and to the popularisation of new words. Here is Trotsky again:

> Notice with what sensibility the languages of civilised nations have distinguished two epochs in the development of Russia. The culture of the nobility brought into world currency such barbarisms as Tsar, Cossack, pogrom, nagaika. You know these words and what they mean. The October Revolution introduced into the language of the world such words as Bolshevik, Soviet, Kholketz, Gosplan, Piatiletka. Here practical linguistics holds its historical supreme court.[37]

Yet one senses an obvious difference between all these examples and many of the efforts at PC language reform. A note of caution is necessary here, for it is clear that many of the most absurd examples are apocryphal. Have you ever actually heard anyone use 'vertically challenged' or 'follicly impaired' other than ironically? Nevertheless there is an element of pompous artificiality present in PC language which positively invites parody. What this derives from is not an attempt to make language reflect real social change but a vast overestimation of the role of language in bringing about social change and the attempt to substitute language reform for real reform. To put the matter sharply the strategy of the Bolsheviks was to win over the mass of workers, soldiers and sailors, storm the Winter Palace and transfer all power to the soviets, and then rename the streets. It was not to imagine that renaming the streets would bring about the revolution.[38] All too frequently PC seems to get this the wrong way round.

The most fruitful sources of positive linguistic change in recent times have undoubtedly been the black movement, the women's movement and the gay movement. The shift from 'coloured' or 'Negro' to 'black' that took place in the 1960s both reflected and signified a great step forward in pride and self assertion. The appropriation of 'gay' was also obviously a progressive step since all that existed before was the clinical (and usually pejorative) 'homosexual' or hate speech, and gay has won very widespread acceptance. 'Homophobia' was also useful as the appropriate naming of a specific bigotry. 'Sexism' contributed by the women's movement, which has generally replaced the more clumsy 'male chauvinism' (also contributed by the women's movement) has served the same purpose as homophobia and has also achieved wide-spread use.

However, probably the most radical successful challenge to existing linguistic practise has been the challenge to the generic use of 'man', mankind' and 'he'. It is a striking fact that before the 1970s everything written by people of every political persuasion (including male and female Marxists) employed this form, but somewhere in the mid to late 1970s this changed quite quickly and everyone who supported the goal of women's equality, which meant virtually everyone on the left, started to write 'people' for 'men' and 'humanity' for 'mankind'. Of course the change was far from universal but in broadly progressive circles it was quite thoroughgoing. It seemed that at the historical moment the issue had only to be raised for substantial numbers of people to alter their prac-tice. This was possible because this particular linguistic reform was a product of a real movement and a real change in the consciousness of millions of women and men which in turn arose from real changes in material conditions and social relations (the influx of women into paid employment, higher education and the professions, the pill, abortion rights). The innovations introduced by the black and gay movement were effective for the same reasons. In addition such changes could be made without making the language pedantic and complex—PC often accom-plishes the opposite (for instance by tokenistically insisting on writing he/she when 'they' would be more readable).

The problem underlying many of the recent PC efforts has been that these real mass movements have receded, leaving a layer of intellectuals stranded in academic or cultural ghettos trying to continue the struggle by purely verbal means and falling over themselves to find linguistic wrongs to be linguistically righted.

The social condition has been reinforced by two other influences which are, at bottom, expressions of the same situation. The first is French philosophy and social theory, deriving from the work of Sansurre, namely structuralism, post-structuralism, deconstructionism, postmodernism et al.[39] This has led to a pervasive and deep seated philosophical idealism according to which (reversing Marx) social consciousness determines social being and language determines social consciousness. A good example of the kind of thinking this has produced is provided by Dale Spender whose book *Man Made Language* has been influential in the language reform project: 'A patriarchal society is based on the belief that male is the superior sex and many of the social institutions and much social practice is organised to reflect this belief.'[40] Note that here society, institutions and social practice are all based on 'belief'. Where this belief comes from is not explained. This has led to claims that language as a whole is male created and male controlled.

These claims are as plainly and simply false as the idea that the human mind created the physical world or that humanity has suffered lamentably from the *idea* of gravity.[41] While some men (essentially ruling class men) can exercise a disproportionate influence on some parts of language and some of its meanings, language as a whole is no more controlled by men as a whole than is the world economy or world culture. It is in the nature of language that it evolves historically through human practice—which includes, albeit in subordinate roles, the practice of women, children, blacks, Jews and everyone else in society.[42]

While it is true that the development of language gave an enormous boost to the development of consciousness and thought, and that the nature of language exercises an important influence on what is thought and what is 'thinkable', it cannot be true that there is no consciousness or thought prior to language or animals would be unable to hunt, cats would not find their way home, chimps could not engage in elementary tool use and babies would not be able to learn language. Nor is it true that language constructs or determines consciousness from nothing. If it were, the project of language reform would itself be inconceivable. There is an ongoing complex interaction between external material conditions, physical and psychological human needs, human social relations and human thought and language. Within this interaction social being— the combination of circumstances, needs and social relations—remains primary.

The development of language is tied to the development of society, reflecting the contradiction and conflict at the root of society, not just the views of the ruling class and their academic followers.

Nevertheless intellectuals have always been drawn to theories that flatter their role and place them at the centre of historical change. What this leads to in practice is such things as the futile attempt to purge English of all negative uses of the word black, as in 'black day', 'black spot', 'blackmail', and 'blacking' (or even non-pejorative uses such as black coffee) or all words with male associations such as 'seminal' or 'seminar' or to replace 'history' with 'herstory' or 'women' with 'wimmin'. The net effect of this fetishism is simply to provide entertainment (at the left's expense) for the press and the occasional refuge for scoundrels, as when certain trade union officials opposed to blacking Timex products because it involved breaking trade union laws claimed they objected to 'blacking' as racist.

What it also fails to understand is that, if people or conditions are renamed or redescribed but reality is not changed, the new name or new description will soon come to take on the old meaning and connotations. Thus a school which practises streaming may decide to rename its A, B and C streams L, M and N, but the children at the school will still tell you that the N class is the 'thickies' class. Similarly the attempt to relabel backward children as 'special needs' or 'children with learning difficulties' or disabled children as 'differently abled' results, in the absence of any deeper change, only in people saying 'special needs' or 'differently abled' and thinking 'backward' or 'disabled'. Worst of all the obsession with language serves to trivialise and discredit anti-racism and anti-sexism in the eyes of many working class people whose exploitation and harsh conditions of life ensure that they have far more serious and pressing things to worry about than pedantic linguistic niceties. In this respect PC can be directly counterproductive, objectively strengthening the reactionary ideas it sets out to combat.

The second more mundane and material influence on PC language reform has been the professional need for jargon. Under capitalism all the elite professions—doctors, lawyers and so on—tend to develop their own jargon incomprehensible to the lay public. Some of this is justified by convenience and/or the need for specific scientific rigour but much of it is elitism pure and simple. It excludes the majority from the professions' deliberations while mastery of the jargon serves as a badge of club membership. The academic world is full of this and Marxist academics are certainly not immune to it. It plays a considerable part in PC language. As Barbara Ehrenreich comments, 'I have seen PC culture in college campuses, chiefly among relatively elite college students or relatively elite college campuses. It amounts to a form of snobbery'.[43]

For socialists with an orientation on the working class any snobbery about how working people, awaking to political consciousness, express themselves is disastrous. This does not mean compromising with racist or sexist ideas but it does mean focusing on what people do and what they think rather than on the formalities of language. The Marxist motto is not, 'In the beginning was the word', but, 'In the beginning was the deed'.

Western culture and the canon

Of all the issues arising in the PC debate in America it is the struggle between the defenders of Western culture and the proponents of multi-culturalism which has probably generated most heat. The European and the North American bourgeoisie has invested a great deal—financially, politically, intellectually—in its particular view of history and culture. This view depicts the 'rise of civilisation' as a more or less linear process beginning in the Middle East (temporarily annexed to Europe for those purposes) and running through Ancient Greece, Ancient Rome, the Middle Ages, the Renaissance, the Reformation and the Enlightenment to present day Western democracy. It depicts all, or almost all, the highest philosophical, scientific and artistic achievements (Homer, Plato, Aristotle, Dante, Michelangelo, Shakespeare, Newton, Mozart, Goethe, Kant, Einstein etc) as lying within this tradition. Until recently this world historical picture has permeated and dominated all education in the West; indeed it remains overwhelmingly dominant to this day. At present, however, it is facing a challenge from within American universities—a challenge mounted in the name of multiculturalism.

This debate has raised a host of issues ranging from the status of scientific knowledge to the origins of Ancient American civilisation—enough to fill volumes with many of the individual controversies requiring specialist knowledge in their own right. All I shall attempt to do here is to offer a brief summary of the multiculturalist case and the outline of the Marxist response to the issue as a whole. The main charges levelled at the canon of Western civilisation are as follows:

(i) That this form of education is inappropriate for a multicultural society and a multicultural student body—it assumes a single, more or less homogenous dominant culture and fails to meet the needs of minority students (for role models, sense of identity, self esteem and so on).

(ii) That this Western tradition is not only inappropriate but false. That its profound Eurocentric bias has distorted the true picture of human development, excluding, downgrading and trivialising the contributions of non-white, non-European cultures.

(iii) That the Western tradition as a whole has been imperialist, racist, 'classist', sexist, homophobic and so on.

(iv) That all, or virtually all, the individual products of this tradition are permeated or at least tainted with racism, sexism and other reactionary ideologies.

On the basis of these charges the conclusions are drawn that both the canon and the curriculum are in a drastic need of revision; that the Western tradition and all its works must be criticised in such a way as to expose its inherent oppressiveness and, if not ousted altogether, at least removed from the centre of the stage and placed on an equal footing with other cultural traditions; that the study of DWEMs (Dead White European Males) must give way, at least partly, to the study of work produced by the oppressed.

Naturally such accusations and proposals have produced howls of outrage from traditionalists and conservatives inside and outside the academy. Where should Marxists stand?

We must begin by recognising the truth of some of the multiculturalist case. It is true that the Western cultural tradition is a tradition shaped by exploitation, oppression, slavery, conquest and so on (although it has also been shaped by resistance to all that, albeit not to the same degree). It is true that the presentation of that tradition in education has been Eurocentric and either explicitly or implicitly racist in its downgrading of all other traditions. It is true that the real history of humanity has been profoundly distorted. It is true that the most outstanding representatives of this tradition are nevertheless the products of this society and that much of their work has been tainted by reactionary ideas and that Kant was a racist, T S Eliot an anti-semite and so on, not to speak of a minor figure like Larkin. It is true also that education and students would benefit from the correction of Eurocentric distortions and the study of Confucius alongside Locke, Rabindranath Tagore as well as Walt Whitman, Ben Okri and Toni Morrison as well as William Golding.

However, we must also recognise that Marxists arrive at this (partial) agreement from a different starting point and with a different methodology from that which is currently dominant within the multiculturalist tendency. Marxists approach culture from a perspective of historical materialism. Culture in all its forms arises from the economic foundations of society—its forces and relations of production. As Engels repeatedly stressed in his letters on historical materialism, the relationship between the economic base and the ideological superstructure is not one of simple reflection or mechanical determination,[44] nevertheless there is always a relation and production remains primary. There is no philosophy, religion or art so rarefied as to be completely detachable from the material conditions in the society of which it is a product. Moreover in a class divided society the dominant culture will always be the culture of the dominant class, of the class which because it controls the means of material production also controls the means of mental production.[45] From this it follows that if the ruling class in society is slave owning then inevitably the culture will reflect this. If the ruling class is imperialist then this will leave its mark on the religion, the literature and the arts. If the society is one in which women are oppressed, sexism will be found in its paintings, its music and its novels.

But from this approach there also follow certain crucial differences with the PC version of multiculturalism. When PCers condemn Western civilisation as aggressive and oppressive they put the accent on Western as if it were an active explanatory category. For Marxists the key category is civilisation. The rise of civilisation—living in the cities—derived from the production of a surplus above what is needed for immediate subsistence and the consequent division of society into classes one of which lived off the labour of the other. Thus civilisation, up to the present, and all its culture have rested on the foundation of exploitation, and therefore are inseparable from aggression, repression, violence and the rest. The historical fact that over the last 500 years the forces of production developed more rapidly in Europe and North America may mean that Western civilisation developed these characteristics to the highest degree—to the level of Auschwitz and Hiroshima—but these characteristics are also to be found in every civilisation based on exploitation and division into classes, that is every society, North, East, South and West that stands between the end of primitive communism and the achievement of socialism. It is therefore futile to condemn Western civilisation in the name of Eastern, African or other civilisations as if war, oppression, slavery and other abominations were not to be found there and it is the temptation to do this which often exposes PC to ridicule, for such claims can so easily be refuted.[46]

Similarly when PCers speak of Western European Male Culture they are stressing categories which are at best secondary and omitting the category which is actually fundamental to explaining contemporary culture, namely bourgeois or capitalist. Of course it is true that capitalism developed first in Europe and Europeans happened to be white and that this gave the white European bourgeoisie an epoch of world economic, political and cultural dominance, but to imagine there is some intrinsic link between whiteness or Europeans and capitalism or dominance is as absurd as imagining there is something peculiarly British about industrialisation or Chinese about gunpowder. It is also an intellectual capitulation to the racist mythology it seeks to combat. Capitalism can develop and has developed on all five continents among people of black, brown or white skins and in the process has given rise to a remarkably similar culture.

Again because PC discourse tends to omit or downplay the categories of capitalism and class it also tends to exaggerate the homogeneity of Western culture and underestimate its contradictions, producing a kind of cultural or even biological reductionism far wider than the economic reductionism of which Marxism is often accused. The idea that the content of every individual's thought or art is mechan-

ically fixed by that individual's race, gender, class or nationality is man-
ifestly false. Blake, Shelley, Rembrandt, Goya and Brecht are all Dead
White European Males, and all have a prominent place in the canon, yet
to imagine that the work of any of them represents an uncritical expression of the status quo or the dominant culture is never to have looked at
it. Indeed the work of all of them contains much that can inspire the
revolt of the oppressed of both sexes and all continents. Even among
writers whose politics were reactionary—the likes of Balzac, Kipling,
Eliot, and Lawrence—elements of a powerful critique of existing
society are present.

Indeed even to speak of Western culture as feudal, capitalist and
imperialist is still an oversimplification. Any class society is a society of
class domination but it is also a society of class struggle. There is
always resistance and the resistance always makes an impact on the
culture. The Bible contains not only, 'Render unto Caesar that which is
Caesar's, but also, 'It is harder for a rich man to enter the kingdom of
heaven than for a camel to pass through the eye of a needle.'

Medieval culture was predominantly feudal aristocratic and religious
but it also contains John Bull's lines, 'When Adam delved and Eve span,
who was then the Gentleman?' Michelangelo worked for the Medicis
and the Pope but his work, for example his Slave sculptures, also gave
extraordinarily powerful expression to the struggle for human freedom.
Eighteenth century English painting was predominantly in the service of
the landed gentry—Gainsborough's *Mr and Mrs Andrews* being the
supreme example—but alongside Gainsborough stands the sharp satire
of Hogarth.

Imperialism has left its mark on the English literary canon from
Robinson Crusoe to *Heart of Darkness* but resistance to imperialism is
by no means absent, think of Wordsworth's sonnet *Toussaint
L'Ouverture*, Swift's *Modest Proposal*, or Yeats' *Easter 1916*.

In the 20th century the United States has been the premier capitalist
country and its culture is inevitably saturated with capitalist values yet
American culture also includes Steinbeck's *The Grapes of Wrath*,
Chaplin's *Modern Times*, Ginsberg's *Howl* and the songs of Joe Hill and
Woody Guthrie and that is without mentioning the black contribution.

Therefore any simplistic rejection either of Western culture as a
whole or of individual writers or artists on the grounds of their colour,
ethnicity, gender or class is foolish in the extreme.

For Marxists this aspect of the PC debate has a familiar ring, for a
similar tendency making similar mistakes arose within our own tradition
after the Russian Revolution. Proletcult, the movement for proletarian
culture, took its stand on the ground of class, not race or gender, but it
fell into the same grandiose rejection of past culture, the same oversimplification of the relation between politics and art and the same illusions

that a new culture could be generated by dogmatic prescription. At the time the foremost Marxist theoreticians, Lenin and Trotsky, firmly rebutted these exaggerated claims and explained that a revolutionary attitude to 'Western'—ie bourgeois—culture meant not throwing it in the dustbin but a long struggle to appropriate its achievements for the benefit of all the exploited and oppressed who have hitherto been denied them.[47]

One relatively new issue which has featured prominently in the PC debate is the question of Afrocentrism. This is an account of historical development advanced by a number of black nationalist writers, such as Molefi Kete Asanta and Leonard Jeffries in opposition to the dominant Eurocentric account. This perspective comes in a number of different versions but its main claims are that Africa is the birthplace of humanity, that Egypt is the birthplace of civilisation, that civilisations that developed elsewhere (Iraq, Greece, China, Central America) were the result of a direct cultural diffusion from Africa and that therefore Africa rather than Europe should rightly stand at the centre of human history.

Of course Afrocentrism is a reaction to the blatant (and covert) racism that has long pervaded Western culture—the kind that refused to believe that the magnificent constructions of the Great Zimbabwe could have been built by Africans. Also some of its claims are true or probably true—that human beings first emerged in Africa, that Egypt is in Africa and that Egypt was one of the earliest civilisations and had a significant influence on Greece. Nevertheless there is an evident defect in the Afrocentrist approach in that it attempts to invert Eurocentrism using many of the same highly ideological and unscientific racial categories. For example there has been heated controversy over the precise skin colour of Ancient Egyptians with European scholarship (particularly in the 19th century) attempting to lighten or whiten the Egyptians, much as Jesus was depicted as white, and Afrocentrists arguing they were black. But from the standpoint of any serious historical account and especially from the standpoint of historical materialism, which rejects completely the idea that culture or civilisation or science or art is the monopoly of any race and rejects the concept of 'race' itself as anything other than a social construction, the skin colour of the Egyptians is a minor empirical question of no more contemporary political significance than whether Ancient Britons painted themselves with dark or light blue woad. Similarly the claim that Ancient Chinese and Ancient American civilisations were African in origin (which both appears improbable and has little or no empirical backing) repeats the Eurocentric error of denying cultural progress to 'other' peoples.

Inverting the myths of the oppressors is not a method confined to Afrocentrism. It has been practised by feminists who try to portray women as the 'caring', 'peace loving' sex, by some vulgar Marxists who glorify the backwardness of the working class and by Stalinists who argued that, since the Western bourgeoisie depicted Stalinist Russia as an evil empire, it must be a workers' paradise. It is always shoddy theory leading only to the substitution of one myth for another.

Having made a critique of Afrocentrism, however, it is also necessary to distinguish between the realm of theoretical struggle and the realm of political struggle, between theoretical compromise and political solidarity—the two are connected but not identical. For example, Malcolm X in his autobiography records his induction into the historical theory of the Nation of Islam according to which whites were a race of 'devils' specially bred on the island of Patmos 6,000 years ago by the evil scientist Mr Yacub.[48] This 'demonology', as Malcolm X himself later called it, is purest nonsense of similar scientific standing to the myth of God creating women from Adam's spare rib. But this in no way alters our political solidarity with Malcolm X as a great fighter for black liberation and our support for him against the racists, the ruling class and the liberals (many of whom doubtless hold more accurate theories of human development). Similarly in many political struggles against racism we have to stand with the Afrocentrists without making concessions to their erroneous theories.

One final criticism must be made of the PC approach to 'Western culture' and the canon. Pigeon holing art, artists and audiences into rigidly circumscribed ethnic, gender or national boxes creates an obstacle to understanding and appreciating one of the most important contemporary cultural trends both in 'high art' and on the streets—namely cultural interaction, borrowing and fusion. In reality cultural fusion is as old as human culture itself, but in the era of world capitalism, international production and global communications its frequency and variety has enormously increased. From the Latin American novel to South African music and Zimbabwean sculpture, cultural borrowing and interaction are at work producing vital artistic innovation. Traditionalists will deplore or dismiss these developments as in a previous generation they condemned jazz, blues and then rock as 'jungle music', but life and art will pass them by. More dangerous perhaps is the threat of absorption, corruption and homogenisation by the Disney/Hollywood (or, for that matter, Bombay) money machine. But it is clear that this rich diversity cannot be defended or encouraged by the mechanical methods of PC. What is required is a genuine internationalism which understands that all culture is a creative human response to the social conditions of people's lives in all their complexity and contradictions.

A note on Britain

So far this article has focused on the PC debate in America but clearly many of its arguments and conclusions are applicable to PC in Britain.

There are however some differences which require comment. In the first place both the controversy and the phenomenon itself have been on a much bigger scale in the US than has been the case or seems likely to be the case in the future in Britain. There are a number of reasons for this: the fact that the left in Britain is more rooted in the working class and its mass organisations; the fact that blacks and other ethnic minorities are a higher proportion in the US and also a higher proportion of the student population and constitute stronger lobbies within bourgeois politics; the fact that the black, women's and lesbian and gay movements have all been bigger in the US.

For all these same reasons PC activities in Britain (and the attacks on them) seem likely to be concentrated in areas such as social work, the probation service, schools (as opposed to universities[49]) and local government and their associated trade unions. These are areas which have attracted left wingers and in which left ideas, especially anti-racist, anti-sexist ideas have had a strong presence. However they are also areas in which educated leftists in the upper ranks of the white collar working class, or the middle class, hold managerial or semi-managerial positions. Thus the temptation arises to attempt to impose anti-racism, anti-sexism and so forth from above by means of administrative regulations. This leads straight to some of the more detrimental features of PC. The problems of PC are particularly acute when the agencies concerned are involved in administering inadequate and declining resources so the tensions between the professionals, seen as representing the state, and their clients are aggravated.

In many ways the controversy surrounding what the media called 'loony left' Labour councils in the 1980s was an example of what today would be dubbed a controversy about PC. Young 'Bennite' Labour councillors were elected full of plans to improve services and fund initiatives for blacks, women, lesbians and gays. The latter usually consisted of a mixture of genuinely progressive policies and a certain amount of PC type tokenism. The Labour councils' failure to resist rate capping and the poll tax left them presiding over worse, not better, services, but clinging to their tokens, which were usually cheap but often irrelevant to most workers white and black, male and female. To put it crudely, it cost less to stick up signs proclaiming the borough a nuclear free zone or to rename a tower block Nelson Mandela House than it does to provide decent street lighting or house repairs. This obviously left the councils open to attack from the right and the press with a good chance of the attacks striking a chord among working class people. Labour's sustained move rightwards has by and large eliminated the left councils and shifted the focus for the PC onto the welfare agencies and the like.

Social work is a good example of an arena in which PC is likely to arise. Social workers are employed by the capitalist state to handle the casualties of exploitation, poverty and unemployment. By 'handling', the state means a combination of help and discipline to maintain social stability. Within this combination the people who become social workers put the emphasis on help (at least subjectively). The state, however, puts the emphasis on social control. Social workers, no matter how well intentioned or left wing cannot escape entirely the disciplinary role they are constrained to play. Most working class people are aware of this and therefore view social workers with deep ambivalence. That social workers make efforts to address this problem is, of course, a step forward. But the nature of their objective position means this is likely to be done in a bureaucratic, dogmatic, top down manner.

One instance which perhaps does not strictly come under the heading of PC but illustrates the dangers was the response by some social services to the problems of child sexual abuse. Obviously social workers were put in an impossible situation, subject to the contradictory imperatives of protecting children and keeping families together—damned if they intervene and damned if they don't. Nevertheless it is clear that in some instances such as Cleveland they overcompensated for past denial, erected a dogma of near universal child abuse and reacted in a way that was disproportionate and extremely insensitive to working class families and children.

Another more evidently PC example is the question of mixed race adoption. A number of social services have taken a position of total opposition to all mixed race adoption, including by mixed race couples. The well meaning justification for this policy is that since black people face racism in this society only black parents can give black children the support they need to deal with this. But behind this argument stand a number of typical PC ideas: that all whites are racist, that 'white culture' and 'black culture' are completely distinct and separate entities and that black culture, at least, should remain so.

This fails to recognise that there are many white adoptive parents who are anti-racists, who are perfectly capable of supporting black children against racism, who will know or learn about black culture, and who will bring up their children proud to be black, just as there also exist black parents who will bring up their children as Uncle Toms. In the meantime, since there is a surplus of black children in need of adoption, children are left in care or institutions. At the same time the 'same race only' policy, by focusing on skin colour instead of attitudes, concedes the right wing racist argument that 'race' is a fundamental and insuparable division in the human species and that black and white cannot live together or fully integrate. Here multiculturalism justifies racial separation and works against class unity, the only real basis for fighting racism.

The National Association of Probation Officers (NAPO) also seems to have gone overboard for PC. Charlie Kimber, in an excellent *Socialist Worker* article on PC, reports:

> *In 1991 delegates to the union's conference were given a handbook outlawing terms like 'paymaster' as sexist and 'fat chance' as sizeist. The next year the national executive ruled out a motion which included the term 'tinkering' on the grounds that it was offensive to gypsies. It added that strike breakers could not be termed 'scabs' because it was offensive to people with skin disorders... NAPO also mobilises language monitors to listen to conference delegates.*[50]

As Charlie succinctly comments, 'This is nonsense'. It also seems likely that it is an attempt to compensate linguistically for the deeply problematic role that probation officers are obliged to play as the soft wing of the judicial system.

Another focus for PC in Britain is the race relations industry—the network of official bodies centred on the Commission for Racial Equality, staffed by people professionally employed to improve race relations and combat racism. Traditionally the race relations industry has been dominated by liberal (or even right wing) paternalist whites and extremely moderate and respectable middle class blacks, but there is also a more radical left wing of the same industry. However, what the left shares with the right is that their anti-racist activity tends to be confined to the committee room. They spend their lives drawing up policies for the health service, the police, education and so on, hardly ever stepping into the streets or the estates to confront racism at the sharp end. Words are, once again, at a premium. The left contends with the right over language, over what the committee should be called, over what its aims and obligations should be and so on. Thus arises a culture obsessed with terminological correctness.

In all of these situations socialists have the task, by no means an easy one, of separating out and supporting every genuine step forward against oppression and discrimination from meaningless and counter-productive tokenism, without giving comfort to the right. An example of how not to respond is provided by Melanie Phillips. In an anti-PC diatribe in the *Observer* she launched into an attack on social work training which employed all the hyperbolic language of the American right wing. So we are regaled with shock-horror reports of 'a corruption of the traditional values of open-minded education', of 'totalitarianism', of 'browbeating into false confessions' and 'vicious intolerance'. In the course of her attack Phillips, like D'Souza and Hughes before her, undoubtedly scores some hits. However, she also roundly condemns social work training courses for being required to deal with 'processes of structural oppression, race, class and gender' and for ensuring students are aware of 'individual and institutional racism and ways to combat both through anti-racist practice'.[51] To this one is forced to reply, what sort of social work course for contemporary Britain would *not* deal with these issues? After all they form part of every A level and GCSE Sociology course.

Above all what is nauseating about Phillip's rhetoric, and also typical of many anti-PC campaigners, is that she writes throughout in tones of expectant martyrdom, congratulating herself on her courage at defying the 'conspiracy of silence'. In fact she is expressing views that will be warmly applauded by every Tory MP, not a few Labour MPs, and every newspaper editor and proprietor and for which she is rewarded by appearing on numerous TV discussion programmes. In short she has played straight into the hands of the right.

As I write these lines Home Secretary Michael Howard is promising to end the right of silence and increase the prison population and Secretary of State for Social Security Peter Lilly is denouncing single parents and foreign scroungers. In the same week the West Midlands police responsible for the incarceration of the Birmingham Six are let off without even facing trial. It all makes a sickening spectacle but in the context of the furore over PC it also seems a useful reminder of who is really threatening 'traditional liberal values', who really displays 'vicious intolerance' and who really gets 'browbeaten into false confessions'.

At the same time a correct identification of the real enemy—the ruling class, its state machine and its political representatives—is the key to avoiding the follies of PC. If we make our primary focus not correcting the language of the student, the teacher and the railway worker but the mobilisation of the same student, teacher and railway worker against the class attacks of that enemy—attacks which are thoroughly material as well as verbal and which include racist, sexist and homophobic attacks—we will not only do more to strike at the roots of racism, sexism and homophobia, but also improve the language and culture of the student, teacher and railway worker in the process.

Notes

1   P Berman (ed), *Debating PC: The Debate over Political Correctness on College Campuses* (New York, 1992), p5. This combines a collection of articles from across the US political spectrum, including pieces by Edward Said, Irving Howe, Stanley Fish, Dinesh D'Souza, and Barbara Ehrenreich. It is therefore an essential source for the debate as it happened in the US.

2   J Searle, 'The Storm over the University', ibid, p86.

3   L Selfa and A Maass, *PC: What's Behind the Attack on Politically Correct?* (Chicago, 1991), p5.

4   D D'Souza, *Illiberal Education* (New York, 1991), p251.

5   'With admirable restraint and civility, D'Souza has written an informative account that provides a rare combination of tough-minded analysis, principled judgements, thoughtful proposals and a humane solidarity'. E Genovese, former Marxist and

author of *Roll, Jordan, Roll: The World the Slaves Made*, quoted on the dust jacket of *Illiberal Education*.

6   Quoted in L Selfa and A Maass, op cit, p2.
7   See N Hentoff, '"Speech Codes" on the campus and Problems of Free Speech', in *Debating PC*, op cit, p2.
8   See I Howe, 'The Value of Canon', in ibid.
9   See E Said, 'The Politics of Knowledge', in ibid. Said also appeared on a late night TV discussion programme chaired by Christopher Hitchens in which he was billed and spoke as an opponent of PC.
10 P Berman, ibid, p5.
11 R Hughes, *Culture of Complaint—The Fraying of America* (New York, 1993), p11.
12 My guess is that such stylistic seduction was responsible for the relatively uncritical review of Hughes' book that appeared in *Socialist Review* (July/August, 1993).
13 I Kristol, 'The Tragedy of Multiculturalism', *Wall Street Journal*, 31 July 1991.
14 See L Selfa and A Maass, op cit, p3.
15 E Genovese, 'Heresy Yes—Sensitivity No', *New Republic*, 15 April 1991, p30.
16 'Faulty Attitudes and Characteristics: Results of a 1989-90 Survey', *Chronicle of Higher Education*, 8 May 1991, A16-A17, cited in L Selfa, op cit, p9.
17 See R Hughes, op cit, p56.
18 Jeffries is the Afrocentrist author of the theory of Ice people (whites) and Sun people (blacks), Rothenburg is the author of a textbook, *Racism and Sexism: An Integrated Study* and professor of philosophy and women's studies at William Paterson College of New Jersey. The Black Faculty Caucus was in a dispute about 'multiculturalism' at the University of Texas in 1990.
19 R Hughes, op cit, p16.
20 This may be an accurate characterisation of the anti-PC campaign as a whole, which has been dominated by the right, but it obviously does not fit someone like Hughes who makes clear his commitment to what he sees as a non-PC multiculturalism and anti-racism. The problem with Hughes is that he takes the very real gains of the 1960s for granted and fails to appreciate the extent to which they were won through struggle, including methods that were extreme or revolutionary. It is this classical liberal error of failing to understand that the cultural and intellectual climate depends not only on rational argument but also on the clash of real social forces, which leads him to write a book which, whatever his intentions, lends aid and comfort to the reactionaries.
21 One example of this approach is M Berbe, 'Public Image Limited: Political Correctness and the Media Big Lie' in *Debating PC*, op cit. Berbe knocks a lot of spots off Messrs Bloom, Kimball and D'Souza but essentially his article does not go beyond being a defence of 'young faculty members' against media misrepresentation. Another is P Rothenburg, 'Critics of Attempts to Democratise the Curriculum are waging a Campaign to Misrepresent the Work of Responsible Professors', ibid.
22 See for example M K Asante, 'Multiculturalism: An Exchange', ibid.
23 E Said, ibid, pp173-174.
24 B Ehrenreich, 'The Challenge for the Left', ibid, p335.
25 The term 'classism' is among the least happy of the PC inventions with its tendency to reduce the material relationship of class exploitation to a mere ideological phenomenon of class prejudice, ie snobbery (a tendency put forward by the bourgeoisie and its apologists including, of course, John Major). It is therefore a theoretical step backwards from the concept of class as such and particularly from 'class struggle'. It should be noted that, whereas socialists

oppose racism and sexism, we support classism in the sense of supporting class consciousness and class struggle.

26   D'Souza repeatedly attacks what he calls 'the victims revolution on campus', but the reality is not revolution but pressure for reform.

27   R Polenberg, *One Nation Divisible: Class, Race and Ethnicity in the United States since 1938* (New York, 1980), p271.

28   Between 1970 and 1977 'the number of black students had more than doubled', ibid, p276.

29   'In 1975, 32 percent of black high school graduates enrolled in institutions of higher learning. In 1988, 28.1 percent of black high school graduates did. During the same period, the white enrolment level *increased* from 32.4 to 38.1 percent'. L Selfa and A Maass, op cit, p12.

30   D D'Souza, op cit, p51. Conservatives like D'Souza use Asian academic 'overachievement' to claim that racism is no barrier to those with the 'right' values and dedication to hard work—both of which are assumed to be 'Asian' cultural traits. In fact, Asian achievement is a function of class. Unlike other racial minorities in the US (ie Blacks and Latinos), the Asian population is a heavily middle class population, owing to US immigration policies which favoured middle class Asian immigrants over working class Asians.
      The 1990 US Census showed that four of 10 Asian families earn more than $50,000 annually and that a similar percentage (39 percent) of Asians 25 years and older have four or more years of college education. Two-thirds of Asian voters voted for Bush in the 1992 election.
      In fact, the University of California admits Asians at a rate of more than three times their representation in Californian high school graduating classes—more than twice the rate a which it admits Latinos. See A Hacker, 'Affirmative Action: The New Look', *New York Review of Books*, October 12, 1989, pp63-65.

31   See L Selfa and A Maass, op cit, p10.

32   The extent of white dominance of American universities in the past is well symbolised by the fact that Harvard, the oldest and most prestigious of all the colleges, has only had two tenured black professors in more than three centuries.

33   L Selfa and A Maass, op cit, p17.

34   N Hentoff, '" Speech Codes" on Campus and Problems of Free Speech', *Debating PC*, op cit.

35   S Fish, in *Debating PC*, op cit, pp231-232.

36   L Trotsky, *The Revolution Betrayed* (London, 1967), p104.

37   L Trotsky, *In Defence of the October Revolution* (London, 1971), p28.

38   It should be noted that the Bolsheviks did not get around to giving even themselves the politically correct name of Communist Party until well after the revolution.

39   For a Marxist critique of these tendencies see A Callinicos, *Is There a Future for Marxism?* (London, 1982) and *Against Postmodernism* (Cambridge, 1992).

40   D Spender, *Man Made Language* (London, 1980), p1.

41   See K Marx and F Engels, *The German Ideology* (London, 1985), p37.

42   It is hard to think of a more marginalised and oppressed group than the gypsies, yet the argot of my home town, Portsmouth (and Portsmouth is not alone on this) contains numerous Romany words which are widely used in the working class: dinlo (stupid), chary (child), mush (bloke), chore (steal), bok (luck or bad luck), kushtee (good, OK).

43   B Ehrenreich, in *Debating PC*, op cit, p335.

44   See for example, Engels to J Bloch, 25 Sept 1890, in *Marx, Engels, Selected Works II* (Moscow, 1962), p488.

45   See K Marx and F Engels, op cit, p64.

46   D'Souza and Hughes are both able to make great play of African complicity and
     Arab practice in the slave trade (see D D'Souza, op cit, pp76-77, and R Hughes,
     op cit, pp140-147). Indeed Hughes is able to turn the slavery argument round into
     a special merit of the West on the grounds that while 'Africa, Islam and Europe all
     participated in Black slavery...only Europe (including, here, North America)
     proved itself able to conceive of abolishing it (p146). But Hughes misses two
     crucial points again through his focus on culture rather than economics and
     struggle. First, Western abolition of the slave trade and slavery derived not from
     morality but from the transition to industrial capitalism for which slavery is
     unsuited—hence the conflict between the northern industrialist states and the
     Southern plantation based states. Second, he ignores the role of the slave revolts
     such as that led by Tousaint L'Ouverture in San Domingo.

47   See L Trotsky, *Literature and Revolution* (London, 1991), and L Trotsky, *On
     Literature and Art*, (New York, 1970), especially, 'Class and Art', pp63-82.

48   See *The Autobiography of Malcolm X* (Harmondsworth, 1968), pp258-262.

49   The main exception to this and the main instance of PC in higher education has
     been in the upper echelons of the National Union of Students. In recent years the
     NUS conferences and the NUS bureaucracy have been dominated by frantic
     tokenism and identity politics. This has been linked to a move to the right in terms
     of both general politics and student struggles and PC has been used, more or less
     consciously, as a weapon against the revolutionary left to attack direct action or
     any kind of vigorous politics as 'macho' and 'intimidatory'.

50   *Socialist Worker*, 31 July 1993.

51   M Phillips, 'Oppressive Urge to Stop Oppression', the *Observer*, 1 August 1993.

E P Thompson: class struggle and historical materialism

DAVID McNALLY

Edward Palmer Thompson, the greatest Marxist historian of the English speaking world, died in August of 1993. Best known for his masterpiece *The Making of the English Working Class*, Thompson launched a current in Marxist history which restored the exploited and oppressed to their rightful place as makers of history. This emphasis on working class self activity was not merely an academic project; it emerged as part of Thompson's political commitment to freeing Marxism from the terrible distortions of Stalinism, a commitment which originated in the battles of 1956 within the official Communist movement.

Through the Smoke of Budapest: 1956 and the battle against Stalinism

'The Polish and Hungarian people have written their critique of Stalinism upon their streets and squares. In doing so, they have brought back honour to the international Communist movement.'[1] So wrote Thompson in *The Reasoner*, a dissident magazine he and John Saville issued as a challenge to the leadership of the British Communist Party (CP). For Thompson, like many other Communists, the Polish and Hungarian uprisings of 1956 against Stalinism posed a moral and political dilemma: to support their party leaderships, which defended the bloody suppression carried out by Russian troops, or to side with the uprisings of Polish and Hungarian workers. To his lasting credit, Thompson chose the latter course. And he launched a debate in the CP in an effort to confront the party's Stalinist legacy. 'It is time we had this out,' he wrote. 'From start to finish...our leadership has sided (evasively at times, perhaps) with Stalinism.' Against the crimes of Stalinism,

Thompson advocated a 'socialism of free people, and not of secret speeches and police.'[2]

The experience of 1956 left an indelible mark on Thompson's political outlook. This was overwhelmingly a positive thing. Against an abstract, mechanical system of thought and politics which paraded itself as Marxism, Thompson sought to restore to Marxism its commitment to the concrete struggles of actual men and women. Flesh and blood working people, their self activity, their resistance to oppression, their victories and defeats—all these were to be reinstated as the heart and soul of socialist theory and politics. Precisely this—commitment to the actual struggles of real people—was what Stalinist politics had buried beneath a dead weight of dogma and bureaucratic edicts. 'Stalinism', Thompson argued, 'is socialist theory and practice which has lost the ingredient of humanity.' Stalinism begins, he claimed, with a line set according to the interests of the bureaucratic party leadership, rather than with a concrete analysis of the actual social reality in which people live, work and struggle. Everything is then subordinated to proving the infallibility of this line. 'Instead of commencing with facts, social reality, Stalinist theory starts with the idea, the text, the axiom: facts, institutions, people must be broken to conform to the idea.' It follows that Stalinism operates as a sort of 'mechanical idealism' in which human beings are mere playthings to be manipulated according to the overriding idea which the party claims as truth.[3]

Central to Thompson's political and theoretical project was the battle against the reifying tendencies of bourgeois thought—its propensity to reduce human beings, their social relations, and their historical experiences to relations between things which utterly determine social life. As a form of socialism which had liquidated 'the ingredient of humanity', Stalinism had lost sight of the fact that, however conditioned they might be by objective circumstances, ultimately human beings made their own history.

Thompson's rebellion against Stalinism was fought under the banner of 'libertarian communism'.[4] And it was this perspective, with its insistence upon the living struggle of working people for their self emancipation, which decisively shaped his most important pieces of historical writing and which made his work a vital contribution to the renewal of Marxism.

The Making of the English Working Class: Marxist masterpiece

No reader of Thompson's greatest work, *The Making of the English Working Class* (1963), can fail to be struck by its author's passionate insistence that in making history working people also make themselves. This theme, working class agency and self activity, sharply distinguished the *Making* from so much of what had passed for Marxist historical analysis during the period in which Stalinism dominated the left internationally.[5] Indeed, in the famous preface to that work, Thompson spelt out the unique character of his approach to the issues of class and class struggle, implicitly contrasting it with the mechanical materialism of Stalinist historiography.

He had chosen the 'clumsy' notion of the *making* of the English working class, Thompson explained, in order to depict 'an active process, which owes as much to agency as to conditioning'. Class, he insisted, is not a structure or a category; it is 'something which in fact happens (and can be shown to have happened) in human relationships'. And these relationships are 'always embodied in real people in a real context'.[6] Against approaches to history which stress 'great figures' or great material changes—the opening of trade routes, the building of cotton mills—Thompson sought to emphasise the activity of ordinary labouring people as a central factor in the historical process. In doing so he hoped to affirm the fundamental dignity of the masses who make (and have made) history. 'I am seeking', he wrote in a memorable passage, 'to rescue the poor stockinger, the Luddite cropper, the "obselete" hand-loom weaver, the "utopian" artisan, and even the deluded follower of Joanna Southcott, from the enormous condescension of posterity.'[7] These people mattered, Thompson insisted, because the English working class had been made not just by patterns of capital accumulation and market competition, but also by the ideas, aspirations and struggles of workers striving to influence the conditions of their lives.

In its effort to restore meaning to the activity of the common people, the *Making* regularly takes aim at the reifying tendencies of mainstream historical analysis. When history is presented as a series of interlocking events each of which is fully determined by the other, 'we arrive at a *post facto* determinism,' Thompson writes. 'The dimension of human agency is lost and the context of class relations is forgotten.' And, as so often, he gives us a beautifully illustrated example of how events are saturated with the social relations of class:

> *The raw fact—a bad harvest—may seem to be beyond human election. But the way that fact worked its way out was in terms of a particular complex of human relationships: law, ownership, power. When we encounter some sonorous phrase such as 'the strong ebb and flow of the trade cycle' we must be put on our guard. For behind this trade cycle there is a structure of social relations, fostering some sorts of expropriation (rent, interest, and profit) and outlawing others (theft, feudal dues), legitimising some types of conflict (competition, armed warfare) and inhibiting others (trades unionism, bread riots, popular political organisation)...*[8]

It is the recognition that these issues—law, ownership and power—were always contested and never merely given that distinguishes the *Making* as a piece of Marxist history. Thompson refuses to fall for the myth of the working class as essentially passive, as simply reacting to external events which determined its fate. Even when discussing the role of religion—in this case Methodism—in blunting and diverting class struggle, he is careful not to portray working people as mere playthings of religious leaders. 'No ideology is wholly absorbed by its adherents: it breaks down in practice in a thousand ways under the criticism of impulse and experience: the working-class community injected into the chapels its own values of mutual aid, neighbourliness and solidarity', he notes.[9]

Thompson's emphasis on the ideas, aspirations, traditions and experiences of working people has been depicted by some critics as a sort of soggy sentimentalism which glorifies the existing state of consciousness of the working class. There *is* a potential danger here. But the *Making* does not succumb to it. While paying detailed attention to the ideological and political traditions of the English working class, Thompson does not flinch from underlining the shortcomings of many of these. In particular, he discusses the limits of the constitutionalism of the radical movement, its insistence that English law is dedicated to the provision of liberties to all subjects and that those who violate these are acting against the constitution. And he underlines the defects of a petty bourgeois radicalism, quite common in the emerging working class movement, which, rather than attacking capitalist ownership, projected the ideal of a community of small independent owners/producers exchanging equitably and living in harmony. On both these points, he indicts the ambiguous radicalism of William Cobbett, whose writings played an enormous role in the working class movement of the early 19th century. Cobbett, argues Thompson, failed as an ideologist of working class mobilisation because 'he reduced economic analysis to a polemic against the *parasitism* of certain vested interests. He could not allow a critique which centred on ownership.'[10] Indeed, the heroes in Thompson's account are those plebian radicals, often members of the revolutionary underground, who did push towards 'a critique centred on ownership,' a socialist critique which moved towards the idea of common ownership of the means of production.[11]

It is worth underlining this last point. *The Making of the English Working Class* rehabilitates a revolutionary underground of working class radicals, stretching from the 1790s into the Chartist period, whose adherents were dedicated to an insurrection against the British state. This feature of the *Making*, which enraged many of its earliest reviewers, has been forgotten by those critics who condemn its alleged populism and romanticism. Throughout the work, Thompson identifies himself with the plebian radicals of the revolutionary underground. In doing so, he challenged the dominant tradition in British labour history—one which stressed gradualism and constitutionalism. Thompson insists that the revolutionaries were not mad plotters and idle cranks. On the contrary, he argues that at a number of points between the 1790s and 1832—most notably in the autumn of 1831—a mass revolutionary sentiment was percolating within the English working class.[12] The *Making* stands out, therefore, not only because it focuses centrally on the self activity of the working class, but also because it demonstrates that revolutionary ideas and organisation played a vital role in the emergence of the British working class movement.

In defence of history

Much of Thompson's work in the 15 year period after the appearance of the *Making* took the form of a defence of the practice of historical materialism against abstract and schematising tendencies within Marxism. In 1965, two years after the appearance of his great work, he entered the fray against the two most influential editors of the *New Left Review* (*NLR*), Perry Anderson and Tom Nairn.

Thompson had briefly collaborated with the two in the early stages of the *NLR*. In the spring of 1960 the *New Reasoner*, edited by Thompson and John Saville, merged with the *Universities and Left Review* to create the *NLR*. At the beginning the *NLR* was seen as part of a practical political project: the *Review* would be linked to New Left Clubs in an effort to build a new socialist movement in Britain. Inevitably, uncertainty over key questions like revolution or reform and a lack of clarity about the role and nature of a socialist organisation led to the stagnation and demise of the clubs. In 1962 Perry Anderson was appointed to reorganise the *NLR*—which he did with zest, in the process marginalising Thompson and other founders from the centre of the life of the *Review*.

Thompson's disdain for the direction the *NLR* took under Anderson's tutelage found expression in a brilliant essay, 'The Peculiarities of the English' (1965). 'Peculiarities' was a reaction to articles by Anderson and Nairn which tied the crisis of British capitalism and the alleged impotence of the British labour movement to the 'incompleteness' of the country's bourgeois revolution. Britain had made the transition to capitalism, Anderson and Nairn argued, at a time when the bourgeoisie was still economically, politically and culturally subordinate to the aristocracy. Hence Britain's political institutions were never fully revolutionised (witness the retention of the monarchy and the House of Lords), and its bourgeoisie failed to develop into an aggressive and self confident class capable of establishing political and cultural hegemony in society. An impotent bourgeoisie in turn produced a reformist working class movement.

Whereas the revolutionary traditions of the French bourgeoisie shaped
the emerging working class in that country, the absence of a genuine
bourgeois revolution accounted for the non-revolutionary traditions of
British labour.[13]

Thompson reacted with barely concealed rage to this argument. He
tore into the schematism of the Nairn-Anderson thesis, subjecting it to
merciless criticism. Picking up some of the threads of Marx's discussion
in Part Eight of the first volume of *Capital*, Thompson highlighted the
proletarianisation of rural producers and capital accumulation in agricul-
ture as key moments in the transition to capitalism in England. The
development of English capitalism, he wrote:

> ... *was enormously complex and protracted, commencing (for historical con-*
> *venience) with the great monastic sheep farmers of Domesday, and passing*
> *through the enfeeblement of the barons in the wars, the growth of 'free*
> *labour', the enclosure of the sheep-walks, the seizure and redistribution of*
> *Church lands, the pillaging of the New World, the drainage of fens, and,*
> *thence, through revolution, to the eventual acceleration of enclosure and the*
> *reclamation of wastes.*[14]

Anderson and Nairn see none of this, Thompson maintains, because
they have a ready-made schema which precedes historical investigation.
For Anderson-Nairn, the rise of capitalism in England must follow the
French model. If capitalism emerged there largely in the urban trading
and manufacturing centres, then so it should have in England. The fact
that English capitalism had powerful agrarian roots escapes them.
Furthermore, their schematism prevents them from recognising that
agrarian and industrial capitalists were not two utterly distinct species.
Although they did constitute two different groups, they were welded into
a reasonably unified bloc in response to the emergence of the working
class movement in the era of the French Revolution.[15] The industrial
bourgeoisie was not inept; on the contrary, it perceived its common
interests with agrarian capital in defence of capitalist property against
threats from below.

In attacking Anderson and Nairn, Thompson did not consider that he
was simply correcting erroneous interpretations of history. He saw
himself as defending the practice of historical materialism against an
empty formalism which characterised too much Marxist analysis.
'Minds which thirst for a sturdy platonism very soon become impatient
with actual history', he suggested. A decade later, his defence of 'actual
history' against 'platonic Marxism' took the form of a no holds barred
attack on the structuralist Marxism of Louis Althusser.

Thompson's critique of Althusser developed points which had been
made by other writers.[16] What distinguished Thompson's attack, *The*

Poverty of Theory, however, was its fierce polemical tone and its attempt to demonstrate that Althusser's position was saturated with Stalinism. Not surprisingly, Thompson's polemic begins with an assault on the contempt for history that characterises his adversary's project. Thompson quotes the astonishing statement by two British Althusserians that 'Marxism, as a theoretical and political practice, gains nothing from its association with historical writing and historical research. The study of history is not only scientifically but also politically useless.'[17] And he proceeds to demonstrate that Althusser's system is nothing less than the wildest form of idealism.

Central to Althusser's position was the idea that Marxist science could be constructed only at the level of philosophy by means of the pure refinement of concepts. Any contamination of theory by history, any attempt to ground concepts in lived experience, he denounced as 'empiricism'. It followed that Marxist science could be developed only at a conceptual level, by refining concepts by means of other concepts. Thompson had no doubt as to the thoroughly idealist nature of this theoretical operation:

>...*this procedure is wholly self-confirming. It moves wholly within the circle not only of its own problematic but of its own self-perpetuating and self-elaborating procedures... It is a sealed system in which concepts endlessly circulate, recognise and interrogate each other.*

Such a position is neither scientific nor materialist. And Thompson did not shrink from giving it a name. Althusser's theoretical enterprise, he wrote:

>*is a break from disciplined self-knowledge and a leap into the self-generation of 'knowledge' according to its own theoretical procedures: that is, a leap out of knowledge and into theology.*[18]

The tone of Thompson's spirited polemic offended many academic Marxists. Yet Thompson's combination of satire and denunciation with theoretical argument was nothing new in Marxist polemics against idealism—one need only consult the tone adopted by Marx and Engels in a work like *The Holy Family* to see that *The Poverty of Theory* has its place in a long and honourable tradition. But Thompson's essay offended in large measure because of the political and social characterisation of Althusserianism it contained.

Thompson notes the origin of Althusser's work: 1956. And he recognises that Althusser's project was defined by an effort to render the Communist Parties immune from the sort of criticism which was emanating from libertarian communist and socialist humanist quarters. The easiest way to do that was to eliminate human beings from the project of 'Marxist' science. To that end, Althusser sought to bury Marx's concepts of alienation and reification and to reconstruct Marxist science as a philosophy of structures. But Thompson, seasoned in the battles of 1956, understood the political character of Althusser's project. 'We can see the emergence of Althusserianism', he wrote, 'as a manifestation of a general police action within ideology, as the attempt to reconstruct Stalinism at the level of theory.'[19]

How, then, to account for the popularity of Althusserianism among left wing intellectuals? Here Thompson offers merely the sketch of an argument. But it was no less offensive to many academic Marxists for that. For Thompson's suggestion is that Althusser's work struck a chord because of the elitism peculiar to the left leaning middle class intelligentsia. This group, 'indoctrinated by selective educational procedures to believe that their own specialised talents are a guarantee of superior worth and wisdom, are only too willing to accept the role offered to them by Althusser'—that of philosophical guardians of proletarian science. 'Isolated within intellectual enclaves,' Thompson writes, 'the drama of "theoretical practice" may become a substitute for more difficult practical engagements.' Moreover, because it rests upon the same sort of intellectual elitism which dominates academic life generally, Althusserianism is entirely compatible with recognition and promotion in the world of the colleges and universities; 'it allows the aspirant academic to engage in a harmless revolutionary psycho-drama, while at the same time pursuing a reputable and conventional intellectual career.'[20]

Here we encounter one of the most significant features of Thompson's Marxism—his hostility to academicism. Thompson himself had only an episodic and marginal relationship to the British university system. More than this, however, his insistence on working class self activity put him at odds not only with the academic establishment, but also with the elitist traditions of the intellectual left—one of the many things for which he deserves to be remembered.[21]

Limitations: materialism and moral critique

And yet there is something of a paradox here. For Thompson's work has received increasing academic recognition in recent years. To be sure, this is often simply a result of the sheer intellectual power and excitement of Thompson's historical writing. But there is another reason which must be acknowledged: Thompson's work, contrary to its author's intentions, is susceptible to a degree of incorporation into the latest 'radical' intellectual fad—discourse theory.

It is beyond the bounds of this article to engage seriously with this intellectual trend. Suffice it to say that since the mid-1970s the predominant trend among radical intellectuals has been an avowedly *anti-materialist* one. In the name of rejecting 'economism' and 'class reductionism', large numbers of intellectuals have come to believe the idea that society pivots principally around the 'discourses' which organise the way we see the world and act within it.[22] And some of them have claimed an ally in E P Thompson.

This unlikely alliance centres on Thompson's sharp attacks on the Marxist notions of 'base' and 'superstructure'. For Marx and Engels, these concepts were a sort of shorthand for describing the way in which the forces and relations of production in any society—and the way these are expressed in class conflicts—exercise a determining influence on culture and ideologies. But Thompson reacted harshly against the mechanical way in which these ideas were used within Stalinised Marxism. He believed that the idea of a socio-economic base which conditions a cultural and ideological superstructure tended to encourage reifying thought 'wherein blind, non-human, material forces are endowed with volition—even consciousness—of their own'. The result, he argued, is the reduction of 'human consciousness to a form of erratic, involuntary response to steel-mills and brickyards, which are in a spontaneous process of looming and becoming'.[23]

One can hardly fault Thompson for his concern that the base-superstructure analogy could be abused terribly by those prone to mechanical forms of thought and action. Indeed, Engels had warned against just such abuses when he wrote that 'the materialist conception of history has a lot of dangerous friends nowadays, who use it as an excuse for *not* studying history.'[24] Similarly, Trotsky had cautioned that 'an ignoramus, armed with the materialist dialectic...inevitably makes a fool of himself.'[25]

There is little doubt that 'dangerous friends' and 'ignoramuses' loomed large in the theoretical work that issued from Stalinist quarters. But Thompson did more than attack the use to which such people put the base-superstructure analogy. He argued that the analogy itself 'is radically defective. It cannot be repaired. It has an in-built tendency to lead the mind towards reductionism.' And as a corrective to this tendency he insisted that class was as much a cultural as an economic formation and that 'it is impossible to give any theoretical priority to one aspect over the other.'[26]

This argument carried an enormous hostage to fortune. Appealing though it might have been during a period in which vulgar materialism loomed large as a major threat to authentic Marxism, it is singularly ill equipped to respond to the new idealism which dissolves all of social life into language and discourse. Not that Thompson could ever have countenanced the idea of people as free floating entities adopting new identities (or 'subject positions') every time they come within hailing distance of a new discourse. Such a view is utterly foreign to Thompson's hard nosed recognition that people are born into class relations which strongly condition the whole make-up of their lives. In fact, Thompson never relinqished the idea that productive relations occupy a central role in social life. Even in his famous preface to the *Making* he maintains that 'the class experience is largely determined by the productive relations into which men are born—or enter involuntarily.'[27] Similarly, in the midst of one of his sharpest attacks on the base-superstructure analogy, he insists that he is not calling into question 'the centrality of the mode of production (and attendant relations of power and ownership) to any materialist understanding of history.'[28]

Yet how is this insistence on the centrality of the mode of production to social life to be theoretically defended once we have abandoned the idea that some aspects of human existence are more foundational than others? Why privilege class in any account of history, after all, if the experiences out of which class develops—people's positions in a system of social production—are no more basic than anything else to the workings of society? Thompson has no serious answers to these questions. And given this, it comes as little surprise when we find one of his followers arguing that 'we cannot after all establish any logical necessity for the primacy of production in the explanation of social life.'[29] With that concession, however, the whole Marxist project collapses—the idea that class struggle is central to recorded history as much as the notion that working class self activity is the key to overturning capitalist society.

None of this is meant to accuse Thompson of having conspired to aid and abet the decline of historical materialism and the rise of discourse theory. Indeed, Thompson would have recognised the latter, with its elevation of speech and thought above labour, as just another episode of bourgeois elitism. Nevertheless, it must be acknowledged that, in attacking the base-superstructure analogy and the central role Marx accorded economic activity in social life, Thompson unwittingly opened the door to an anti-materialist current in contemporary social theory.[30] Especially where he insists that culture is as determinant as economy, Thompson assisted a trend he would probably have disowned.[31]

This point is brought out clearly by a North American Marxist historian who has taken his inspiration from Thompson's historical writing. While acknowledging the important role played by Thompson and his contemporary Raymond Williams in countering structuralism and vulgar materialism, Bryan Palmer notes nevertheless that 'something was lost in the assimilation of agency and structure, culture and materiality.' And, he continues, since the late 1970s:

> ... the theoretical claims of Thompson and Williams were all too easily incorporated into an emerging orthodoxy...that closed its nostrils to the foul smell

of economism without reflecting on the extent to which it was also, simultaneously, shutting its eyes to materialism. The cultural became the material; the ideological became the real.[32]

It must be acknowledged, in fact, that Thompson exhibited a tendency to slip from materialist to moral-cultural critique. I am inclined to think, ironically, that this slippage owes something to the nature of his critique of Stalinism. For all its moral and political fervour, there was something remarkably imprecise about his attack on Stalinism. Thompson described his as a 'moral critique of Stalinism'—and there is much to be said for that. Whatever its limitations, revolutionary socialists can only applaud a critique which refuses to countenance slave labour camps, show trials, mass murder, a police state regime of lies and crimes against human rights, as authentic forms of socialism. But alongside the vigour of moral denunciation one needs a clear analysis of the nature of the regimes at issue. At no time did Thompson offer the latter. And his gestures towards such an analysis can only be described as feeble. Thus in his polemic against Althusser he writes that 'the Soviet state can only be understood with the aid of the concept of "parasitism".'[33] But writing as a historian of English radicalism, Thompson had alerted us to the shortcomings of just that term. Discussing William Cobbett in the *Making*, for example, Thompson indicts his radicalism for reducing 'economic analysis to a polemic against the *parasitism* of certain vested interests'.[34] Yet in the case of the Russian state that is precisely what Thompson does. Nowhere does he engage with the existing economic analyses of Russia; instead, he restricts himself to a moral critique of parasitism.

This, it seems to me, is the greatest shortcoming of Thompson's political writings: his predisposition to supplant materialist analysis with moral critique. Often these critiques are passionate in the extreme—they fairly ring with indignation. Yet just as often they lack the sort of probing and systematic analysis required if they are to be convincing and if they are to serve as guides to action. One example should illustrate the point.

During the 1970s Thompson became increasingly preoccupied with the growth of the 'secret state' in Britain and its invasions of civil liberties. Understandably, he expressed annoyance with Marxists who considered such questions irrelevant. Yet, in bending the stick against those who were indifferent to civil rights, Thompson tended to lose his critical distance. He praised the rule of law as 'an unqualified human good', as 'a cultural achievement of universal significance', without so much as an acknowledgement of the contradictory character of law and of the fact that it is at least in part an expression of the alienation of people from the state that characterises class society.[35]

Then, in a reckless judgement, Thompson came to a thoroughly pessimistic conclusion about the struggle to defend civil liberties. The

British people, he argued, 'have been drugged into an awe of office', they no longer rise to the defence of their traditional rights.[36] Yet Thompson's 'evidence' for this claim involves no attempt at a materialist analysis of the balance of class forces, the state of the working class movement and the left, and other factors which might influence levels of popular opposition to incursions on civil rights. Instead he offers a superficial piece of cultural commentary: 'The free-born Briton has been bred out of the strain... An operation has been done on our culture and the guts taken out.'[37] Subsequently, in a move reminiscent of Cobbett, Thompson takes up the mantle of constitutionalism by suggesting that he and other 'defenders of civil liberties are attempting to uphold the constitution' against the subversions of 'the law and order brigade'. A similar configuration of moral critique replacing materialist analysis haunted Thompson's analysis of the 'exterminism' which he identified in the new Cold War of the 1980s.[38]

Conclusion: Thompson's enduring contribution

There is a danger that in making these criticisms I will lead some to the conclusion that Thompson, while a Marxist of good intent, has little to contribute to the future of revolutionary socialism. I mean to suggest nothing of the kind. E P Thompson was a giant figure in the development of Marxist history. I do not hesitate for a moment to suggest that he was the greatest figure produced by the British Communist Party Historians Group whose numbers included Christopher Hill, George Rudé, Eric Hobsbawm and Rodney Hilton. And that greatness has principally to do with the unwavering political commitment that animates his work: his insistence upon the centrality of working class self activity to the historical process.

There is in Thompson something of the *revolutionary temper*, a disposition towards finding the cracks within the heavy structures of society which enable agency and self activity to bend history, to shape the direction of things. And it is this which makes the best of his work, whatever its limits, marvellous examples of genuine historical materialism at work. Historical analysis for Thompson is never simply about the past. It is also about recuperating past struggles in order to force open the cracks in history which will allow us to make a better future, one in which the glory and the suffering of past struggles are redeemed by future victories for the oppressed and exploited.

And that is why Thompson matters to us today, and why we should mourn his death. There were limits to Thompson's Marxism, some of which I have touched on in this article.[39] But these do not change the fact that he was on our side, the side of those for whom the revolutionary struggle for working class self emancipation is the cause of the present and the future. The criticisms I have made are meant to overcome weaknesses in certain of the positions he adopted in order to preserve and extend the essential thrust of his work. Thompson, I think, would have been the first to understand that his work would be taken up and transformed by others fighting different battles than he. 'What we may hope', he once wrote, 'is that the men and women of the future will reach back to us, will affirm and renew our meanings.'[40] There is much to reach back for in the writings of E P Thompson, and much that deserves to be affirmed and renewed.

Notes

1   E P Thompson, 'Through the Smoke of Budapest', *Reasoner: A Journal of Discussion*, November 1956, as reprinted in D Widgery, *The Left in Britain 1956-1968* (Harmondsworth, 1976), p71.

2   Ibid, pp67, 72.

3   Ibid, pp70, 69.

4   Commitment to the idea of 'libertarian communism' is a constant throughout Thompson's writings. See, for instance, 'A Communist Salute' in the last issue of the *Reasoner* (Spring 1960), as reprinted in D Widgery, op cit, pp90-91; his reference to himself as 'a historian in a libertarian Marxist tradition', in E P Thompson, *Writing by Candlelight* (London, 1980), p166; and his renewed discussion of 'libertarian communism' in his *The Poverty of Theory and other Essays* (London, 1978), p380. Usually this term is used interchangably with that of 'socialist humanism.'

5   Indeed, the exceptions to this rule were generally works which came from within the Trotskyist tradition. One wonderful example is C L R James, *The Black Jacobins*, first published in 1938.

6   E P Thompson, *The Making of the English Working Class* (New York, 1963), p9.

7   Ibid, p12.

8   Ibid, p205.

9   Ibid, p392.

10   Ibid, p757.

11   See, for example, Thompson's discussion of Thomas Spence and his followers as well as his treatment of the radical working class Owenites. For more on these groups, see my discussion in *Against the Market: Political Economy, Market Socialism and the Marxist Critique* (London, 1993), ch 4.

12   Ibid, pp808, 816-817.

13   Anderson returned to his thesis 25 years later, developing it in a form in which its reformist implications became much sharper. See his 'The Figures of Descent', *New Left Review* 161 (January-February 1987). For critiques of this article and its earlier formulation see C Barker and D Nicholls (eds), *The Development of British Capitalist Society: A Marxist Debate* (Manchester, 1988); E M Wood, *The Pristine Culture of Capitalism* (London, 1991); and A Callinicos, 'Exception or Symptom? The British Crisis and the World System', *New Left Review* 169 (May-June 1988).

14   E P Thompson, 'The Peculiarities of the English', in *The Poverty of Theory* (op cit), p41. Compare this description with that by Marx, *Capital*, vol 1 (Harmondsworth, 1976), p895.

15   Ibid, p45.

16   See for example N Geras, 'Althusser's Marxism: An Assessment', and A Glucksmann, 'A Ventriloquist Structuralism', both in *Western Marxism: A Critical Reader* (London, 1977).

17   B Hindess and P Q Hirst, *Pre-Capitalist Modes of Production* (London, 1975), p312.
18   E P Thompson, *The Poverty of Theory* (op cit), pp204, 225.
19   Ibid, p323
20   Ibid, pp377, 376-77, 378. Unfortunately, Thompson's fine discussion here is marred by his underestimation of the events of 1968 and the impact they had in creating genuine revolutionaries around the world.
21   Indeed, Thompson produced one of the finest caricatures of academics yet penned. In his short book, *Warwick University Ltd: Industry, Management and the Universities* (Harmondsworth, 1970), pp153-155, he provides a marvellous discussion of 'the species *Academicus Superciliosus*' who is 'inflated with self-esteem and perpetually self-congratulatory as to the high vocation of the university teacher'. I am grateful to Bryan Palmer for drawing this passage to my attention.
22   For helpful discussions of some of the intellectual trends at work here see R Bradbury, 'What is Post-Structuralism?' *International Socialism* 41 (Winter 1988); B D Palmer, *Descent into Discourse: The Reification of Language and the Writing of Social History* (Philadelphia, 1990); and A Callinicos, *Against Postmodernism: A Marxist Critique* (New York, 1990).
23   E P Thompson, 'Socialist Humanism: An Epistle to the Philistines', *The New Reasoner: A Quarterly Journal of Socialist Humanism* 1 (Summer 1957), pp113-114.
24   F Engels, *Letters on Historical Materialism 1890-94* (Moscow, 1980), p7.
25   L Trotsky, *Notebooks, 1933-1935: Writings on Lenin, Dialectics, and Evolutionism* (New York, 1986), p111.
26   E P Thompson, *Folklore, Anthropolgy and Social History* (Brighton, 1979), pp18, 21.
27   E P Thompson, *Making* (op cit), p9.
28   E P Thompson, *Folklore* (op cit), pp17-18.
29   D Sayer, *The Violence of Abstraction: The Analytic Foundations of Historical Materialism* (Oxford, 1987), p148. It comes as little surprise that Sayer has now adopted whole chunks of the views of Max Weber and Michel Foucault in his recent accounts of the workings of modern society.
30   For Thompson's characterisation of Marx as guilty of a sort of economic reductionism see 'Peculiarities' (op cit), p83; *The Poverty of Theory* (op cit), pp257-60; and *Folklore* (op cit), p19.
31   For one such formulation see E P Thompson, *Folklore* (op cit), p21.
32   Palmer (op cit), p210. For Palmer's tremendous debt to Thompson see his *The Making of E P Thompson: Marxism, Humanism and History* (Toronto, 1981).
33   E P Thompson, *Poverty* (op cit), p241.
34   E P Thompson, *Making* (op cit), p757.
35   E P Thompson, *Whigs and Hunter: The Origin of the Black Act* (New York, 1975), pp266, 265.
36   E P Thompson, 'The End of an Episode', *New Society* (13 December 1979), p608. Note the irony in Thompson talking of a people being drugged when what characterises his historical writing is the insistence that the common people are never fully absorbed into the ideological universe of their rulers.
37   Ibid.
38   E P Thompson, *Writing by Candlelight* (op cit), p210. As always, Thompson's work in this area was distinguished by tremendous passion and enthusiasm. Yet his analysis, set forward in an essay entitled 'Notes on Exterminism, the Last Stage of Civilisation', *New Left Review* 121 (May-June 1980), faltered at crucial points. The essay displays great descriptive powers, as when he discusses the reciprocal logic that binds America and Russia in the arms race. Yet towards the end he claims that 'exterminism itself is not a "class issue": it is a human issue.'

At a purely descriptive level, this is obviously true: nuclear devastation would not discriminate on the basis of class. But analytically and strategically this begs key questions as to whether there is a systemic economic and political logic to the arms race, and whether this could be eliminated without overturning the prevailing class relations of society.

39 For an insightful discussion of the roots of these weaknesses see D Hallas, 'How Can We Move On?' *Socialist Register* 1977, pp6-8.

40 E P Thompson, *Poverty* (op cit), p234.

Jazz—a people's music?

CHARLIE HORE

Introduction

Jazz music has become one of the 20th century's most important and enduring art forms. Yet it survives today in a paradoxical state. On the one hand, the audience for jazz is now larger and more diverse, both socially and geographically, than ever before. Millions of people who don't see themselves as jazz fans regularly listen to live jazz, and most people who regularly buy records or CDs own some jazz. Pubs and bars which feature live music will often have jazz one night, rock the next, and folk the night after; and much the same audience will turn up to hear all three.

On the other hand, jazz as a constantly innovative and evolving art-form is in decline, and has been for the last 20 years. Throughout the 1970s and the 1980s, there were no fundamental developments in the music on the scale of bebop or 1960s 'new jazz'. During that period not one new musician emerged who even remotely approached the stature of figures like Louis Armstrong, Duke Ellington, Charlie Parker, Miles Davis or John Coltrane.[1] This is in no way intended to denigrate the many fine artists playing today; it is rather to state the simple fact that jazz has lost its position at the leading edge of musical development to other musical forms.

The point of this article is to attempt an explanation of this decline by looking at the ways in which jazz and other forms of black music grew out of the black American experience,[2] and how these musical forms have changed as a result of changes in black lives and experiences. Trotsky argued, in *Literature and Revolution*, that:

> ...art should, in the first place, be judged by its own law, that is, by the law of art. But Marxism alone can explain why and how a given tendency in art has originated in a given period of history; in other words, who it was made a demand for such an artistic form and not for another, and why... New artistic needs or demands for new literary and artistic points of view are stimulated by economics, through the development of a new class... Artistic creation is always a complicated turning inside out of old forms, under the influence of stimuli which originate outside of art.[3]

I want to argue that this method can be extended to the formation of black American culture, in the very specific circumstances of slavery and post-emancipation institutionalised racism. In and of America, yet shut out from American society proper, blacks created a culture (in the widest sense of a way of life) which drew both from African cultures and the European ways of life forced on them. As Leroi Jones put it, in his seminal *Blues People*,

> ...the ugly fact that the Africans were forced into an alien world where none of the references or cultural shapes of any familiar human attitudes were available is the determinant of the **kind** of existence they had to eke out here: not only slavery itself but the particular circumstance in which it existed. The African cultures, the retention of some parts of these cultures in America, and the **weight** of the stepculture produced the American Negro...the development of African music to American Negro music (a **new** music) represents to me this whole process in microcosm.[4]

Just as black religions took the forms of Christianity and evolved into something neither European nor African, but rather a black American synthesis of the two, so black music developed as a synthesis of the many musical forms and traditions available. This gave black musical traditions from their earliest days both a dynamism and an ability to absorb new influences, which helps to explain why black American music has been among the most creative and the most influential musical forms of this century.

From this it follows that jazz cannot be understood in isolation from other forms of American black music. The lines drawn between jazz, blues, gospel, rhythm and blues and other forms are largely ones imposed by white critics.[5] The only real distinction recognised by musicians and their audiences for much of this century was that between sacred and secular music. Even here the number of artists who have moved between one and the other suggests that this was a highly permeable boundary.[6]

New Orleans and beyond

The rise of jazz, as a distinct branch of black music, reflected profound changes in black life at the turn of the century. It was an urban music, centred on New Orleans, New York and Kansas City, not the Mississippi Delta or the Alabama cottonfields. It was played by musicians who aimed to make a living from it (unlike the vast majority of blues or gospel singers). And it was a music made for the poor, derided as not respectable by the vast majority of the black middle classes. It arose, in other words, out of a new black working class with money to spend on entertainment who wanted (or were ready to listen to) something different to the music of the countryside they had left behind.

It's in that sense that the term 'a people's music' fitted jazz in its earliest years. It changed and developed as black workers' lives changed, because it was a music rooted in the black working class ghettos, drawing its inspirations from everyday black life.

This is not to argue that it was somehow a 'working class culture', existing outside of and in opposition to capitalist society. The business—sheet music, recording and all but the smallest venues—was entirely run by whites. And the small numbers of middle class blacks contributed disproportionately to the music's development from its earliest days. Nevertheless, as Eric Hobsbawm argued in *The Jazz Scene*:

> ... the crucial factor in the development of jazz, as of all American popular music, the factor which more than any other accounts for the unique American phenomenon of a vigorous and resistant folk-music in a rapidly expanding capitalist society, is that it was never swamped by the cultural standards of the upper classes.[7]

As we will see later, this is a historically specific description which, beyond a certain period, cannot be sustained. But as an analysis of the music in its formative years, it is of great importance. To give just one example: when you listen to the astonishingly explicit (if you understand the slang) sexual and drugs references used by women blues singers in the 1920s and 1930s, it is clear that this was a music never intended for white (or respectable black) ears.[8] The white capitalists who dominated the industry from its earliest years saw it solely as a way of making money. Apart from occasionally toning down the most explicit sexual references, they never made the slightest attempt to control its content. It was simply assumed that the musicians knew what would sell and could produce it on demand (not until the 1950s did any record company even pay musicians for rehearsal time).

Many influences went into the making of jazz, including many elements of European classical and folk music, the former brought by middle class blacks denied entry into the world of concert music. But it was rooted above all in the blues. Blues was a loose and flexible folk form that became codified into the 'traditional' 12 bar blues in the early years of this century. More than other black musical forms it kept crucial elements from African music, in particular the 'blue notes' —pitches which lie between the notes of the classical European scale. While other influences have come and gone, blues has been the seminal influence on jazz since its inception.

Contrary to various claims, no one 'invented' jazz. It emerged at around the same time in a number of different places. But from the early years of this century New Orleans was its crucial seed bed, as the largest and fastest growing city in the south with innumerable opportunities for working musicians—bars, brothels and marching bands among others.

The music quickly spread far and wide as the conditions that had produced jazz came into being in other, northern, cities. Hobsbawm estimated that on the eve of the Depression there were some 60,000 jazz bands and almost 200,000 professional musicians.[9] Its spread followed the first great black migration from the south, which began around 1916 (as jobs opened up due to the war) and continued without interruption until the Depression.

The newborn recording industry greatly facilitated jazz's expansion. Record sales leapt from 27 million in 1914 to 100 million in 1921,[10] and continued to rise throughout the 1920s. Although most of the music which fuelled the 'Jazz Age' was made by whites watering down the music to the point where a white audience would find it palatable, by the mid-1920s the record companies had discovered a substantial black audience. 'Race' labels were founded, advertised only in black papers and sold only in black areas, which sold massive numbers both of blues and jazz records.

And as the music spread, it developed and changed greatly. Listening to Louis Armstrong playing with King Oliver in 1923, and his Hot Fives and Hot Sevens in Chicago in 1927, is almost to listen to two different people. The later music is crisper, faster, more complex and inventive, and clearly represents a challenging of boundaries, a search for different things to do both with the instrument and with other musicians. The distinctive 'New Orleans' style died away quite quickly, although it underwent innumerable revivals, usually by whites reacting against newer developments in jazz.

One of the crucial defining characteristics of jazz is its search for the new. As a music of individual and collective self expression, which stresses each player working out a personal voice and style, it has always striven to deepen its language and move beyond previous boundaries. That development has always been collective, musicians learning with and from each other. A constant tension has thus run through the history of jazz between its function as dance music and its drive to innovate, which has led different schools to go both away from and back to mass audiences.

That drive for self expression and exploration makes jazz pre-eminently a music that voices both emotions and ideas. There's no space here to address the question of how music does this (and I'm far from qualified to attempt a definitive answer), but one point is important. Although early jazz grew up as entertainment, as a music to relax to and escape from the frustrations of everyday life, it necessarily reflected in its tone, language and emotions what it was that its audience wanted to escape from. It became both an expression of alienation and of attempts to overcome it.

Jazz history is conventionally written about as a series of schools— New Orleans, big band, swing, bebop and so on. As a rough template, this does capture the sense of progression in jazz, but it should be noted that this is a very imperfect way of describing jazz's diverse history. All the 'schools' were named by white critics, not the musicians themselves, and they never simply followed a linear progression—as one came into being, the previous one died. Rather, different schools survived side by side. And many of the most important musicians—Art Tatum, Miles Davis and Sonny Rollins, for example—cannot easily be fitted into that framework.

Kansas City to bebop

The Depression of the late 1920s dealt jazz a mortal blow, as unemployment and poverty hit black workers even harder than whites. Dance halls closed down, records stopped selling and promotors stopped booking tours. Black music didn't disappear (sales of Bessie Smith's records kept the giant Columbia Records solvent through the late 1920s)[11] but there wasn't enough work for even a small fraction of the musicians who had been playing in jazz's heyday. There were exceptions, and the major one was Kansas City, which was to produce an enormous number of the most influential musicians of the 1930s and 1940s, among them Lester Young, Ben Webster, Count Basie and Charlie Parker.

The reasons for this were very largely economic. Kansas City had long been the dominant business and entertainment centre for a massive area of the south west. As such it had been a major jazz centre, second only to New Orleans, since the First World War. It also had the dubious distinction of being run by one of the most corrupt political machines ever, that of Boss Prendergast, who ran Kansas City as though Prohibition simply didn't exist. One of the side effects of Prohibition was that in many cities the mob effectively ran the town hall; in Kansas City the town hall was the mob. This produced a massive entertainment district full of opportunities for musicians, and one which, as the depression deepened, pulled in musicians from all the surrounding states.[12]

The Kansas City musicians developed a particular big band style (swing) which emphasised both strongly rhythmical ensemble playing, and a fast and fluent solo expertise. Their crucial technical innovation was that the drummers laid down the underlying beat on the hi-hat, rather than the bass drum as previously, thus making for a looser, suppler and more 'swinging' (that indefinable but essential quality) form of music. 'Cutting sessions' in which musicians tried to outplay and outlast one another, while others looked on and learnt, were regular events in the clubs late at night, and immensely important training sessions. In effect, they worked as a hothouse of musical development and innovation.[13]

Swing was popularised through eastern tours, in particular by the Count Basie band, from the mid-1930s onwards, and it became the popular music of the day with astonishing rapidity. By 1939 fully 85 percent of all records sold were of swing bands.[14] The music's explosive popularity was due above all to the American economy's recovery from the Depression, creating once again a mass audience with the money to pay for popular entertainment, but it was fuelled by two developments which enormously increased the potential audience: radio and the jukebox.

Although radio networks had been expanding since the mid-1920s, it was only after the depression that radios became cheap enough for most workers to buy (in 1926 a mere 5 million homes had radios).[15] The jukebox similarly caught on in the same period—by 1937 there were some 150,000 jukeboxes across the USA.[16]

Although swing had been entirely a black development, it quickly attracted a host of white imitators. Some—Benny Goodman, Woody Herman, and Tommy Dorsey for example—were genuinely excited by what they saw as a new, vibrant music, and their playing demonstrated a real ability to learn from black innovations (though Goodman was the only white band leader who actually employed black musicians). The majority were simply jumping on a bandwagon. Good or bad, it was the white bands who made the real money out of the swing boom. It wasn't the first time that a black music had been popularised by whites (ragtime), or the first time that white imitators had taken over and sanitised jazz. But it was the first time that big money had been involved.

Revulsion against this white takeover was one of the key factors behind the rise of bebop, the most political form of jazz up to this point.

The young musicians who pioneered bebop—Charlie Parker, Dizzy Gillespie, Thelonious Monk, Kenny Clarke and Charlie Christian —had ended up in New York after going through various of the big bands. They wanted, as one of them put it, to 'play something that they can't steal.'[17]

Bebop was marked by two crucial technical innovations. One was rhythmic—taking the underlying beat from the hi-hat to the cymbals, allowing them to play in a faster and more rhythmically diverse style than the previous generation. The other was Charlie Parker's discovery of a completely new set of harmonies to play on conventional chord changes. The combination of the two made bebop the most profound revolution in jazz since Armstrong in the 1920s, and arguably a more important one. It also marked a definitive break with all previous jazz schools—practically no one from any of the older schools ever learned to play bebop.

Bebop's ranks were filled by refugees from the big bands, as America's entry into the Second World War tore many of them apart. Many bands lost key players to the armed forces, while blackouts, petrol rationing and the draft similarly closed many of the biggest dance halls. The smaller bebop bands were cheaper to book and to record (particularly as they played original material, whose copyright could be bought cheaply in the studio). The big bands' decline helped to create a niche for bebop to flourish in.

The politics of bebop

Bebop both prefigured and was shaped by radical changes in black lives during the war. The exodus from the south began again, in even bigger numbers, as jobs opened up in the defence industries of the north, the midwest and California, and almost a million blacks were drafted into the armed forces. For the American ruling class, the Second World War was an all-out war, and they had to fully utilise spare black and female labour, both in defence industries and the armed forces. Leroi Jones noted, for instance, that 'while the number of Negroes [in the armed forces] more than doubled, the number of commissioned officers increased almost eight times.'[18]

The contradiction between the rhetoric of a 'war for democracy' and blacks' centrality to the war effort, and the racism they found in the defence plants and the armed forces produced both a burning resentment against racism, and a confidence and determination that it could be fought. The war years saw the massive March on Washington movement, mass black and white union demonstrations against racism in industry, and innumerable confrontations between black soldiers and racists. This pressure from below forced Roosevelt in 1941 to formally ban segregation throughout the armed forces and industry. Though never fully implemented, it was a symbolic victory of immense importance.[19]

Most importantly of all, as the Chicago and New York race riots of 1943-44 dramatically showed, blacks were willing to fight back. Bebop was powered by, and spoke to, that new spirit of defiance. When Charlie Parker titled one of his most famous recordings *Now's The Time*, it was taken to mean just that: now's the time to end racism, '...so I have been assured by every black musician with whom I have ever discussed the question', Frank Kofsky asserted (though Parker himself never said as much).[20]

Both as a music and in the stances taken by the individual musicians, it reflected that new confidence and self assertiveness: more than any previous form, it stressed the individual soloist, his ideas and his feelings. And in going back to the blues as the roots of jazz, it stressed that this was a black music. As Ross Russell put it:

> *For urban black people of his generation, Charlie* [Parker] *was a genuine culture hero. The revolutionary nature of his music was explicit. He had rephrased Negro music without altering its essential truth and purity. Implicit in his lifestyle was defiance of the white establishment...every episode in the cumulative legend of the Bird, however ineffectual and childish, was seen as a blow struck against the forces of oppression. In the mid-1940s there was no Martin Luther King Jr., no Malcolm X... In a sense Charlie was a fore-runner of those militant figures of the political arena. He was completely non-political, in fact never in his lifetime so much as cast a ballot... Charlie Parker was the first angry black man in music.*[21]

Leaving aside the hyperbole, and the equation of 'political' with voting, this is a useful summary of the strengths and weaknesses of bebop as revolt. For while it's true that bebop articulated both the anger and the confidence of many urban blacks, for the musicians their opposition was expressed in purely personal ways: not acting by the rules, putting on the squares. (When Charlie Parker met Jean-Paul Sartre in a Paris nightclub in 1949, his opening line was, 'I'm very glad to have met you, Mr. Sartre. I like your playing very much.' Sartre's reply is not recorded.)[22]

That stance limited bebop's audience. Bebop was very much a musicians' music, one which made no concessions to the audience: those who were hip would dig, the squares would not. And their definition of 'squares' extended beyond most of the white world to include those blacks (including most older jazz musicians) who found bebop too challenging or too difficult. Louis Armstrong, for instance, famously dismissed it as 'Chinese music'.

Material reasons also limited bebop's audience. The American Federation of Musicians imposed a recording ban in 1942, to get musicians paid proper royalties for radio and jukebox plays. The 'strike' (in reality imposed entirely from above) ended in partial victory in 1944, when the last big record labels signed new contracts. Yet despite the ban, the value of record sales leapt from $50 million in 1941 to $109 million in 1945,[23] as the companies reissued their backlist to stay afloat. As a result, two key years in bebop's evolution went unheard by the vast majority of blacks.

Yet the recording ban wasn't the primary reason why bebop remained a minority black taste, probably having as large a white audience as black. Far more important were two new strands of black music that arose during the war, aimed specifically at the new black working class: Chicago rhythm and blues, and the 'jump' music of bandleaders such as Cab Calloway, Wyonie Harris and Louis Jordan. (The 'jump' bands had been around since the late 1930s, but achieved their greatest popularity during the 1940s.) Although they were among the most popular jazz based bands ever, they are rarely given the importance they deserve in jazz histories.[24]

Both forms stressed showmanship and entertainment, and were played explicitly as dance music, which bebop was not. And both were assiduously promoted by the independent black record labels and radio stations which mushroomed in the immediate post-war years. Both were also seminal to the later rise of rock'n'roll, but that's another story.

Neither rhythm and blues nor jump music were ever explicitly political, in the sense of expressing opposition in their lyrics, but their brash and confident styles gave expression to the new moods, attitudes and expectations which had grown among blacks during the war years, and did so in a far more accessible manner than bebop. There was no necessary opposition between the two: many people happily listened both to Charlie Parker and to Muddy Waters, but the point matters because we can't understand developments in jazz without understanding what else was happening in black music at the time. Jazz was a form of black musical expression, but not always the most important or the most popular one.

It has often been argued that jazz never had a mass black audience, blues and rhythm and blues being always far more popular. There is no way of proving or disproving this for the 1920s and 1930s, when live performances and later radio were the main ways in which music was heard, but in any case it misses the point that for much of this period there was no great distinction between the two. The argument also confuses 'mass' and 'majority'—the jazz audience was probably never a majority of urban blacks, but that doesn't mean that it didn't have a substantial audience. From the later 1940s onwards, however, there was a real divergence among musicians: practically none of the Chicago bluesmen had any jazz background, and very few jazz musicians ever played with them. Although that same divergence began to appear among audiences, it remained the case that jazz retained a large black audience, even if smaller than that for rhythm and blues, until the mid-1960s.

Inside jazz, bebop and the various reactions to it had an enormous influence on the two dominant schools of the 1950s—cool and hard bop. Although the 'cool school' is conventionally dated from Miles Davis's *Birth of the Cool* recordings of 1949 and 1950 (which were only released under that name in 1957), it was overwhelmingly a movement of white musicians, based mainly on the American West Coast, where there was only a very weak black jazz tradition.

As the cool school developed, it became increasingly marked by a rejection of the blues as jazz's major source, looking more and more to European sources and classical influences, in an attempt to gain a respectability for jazz by presenting it as another form of concert music. Politically, it signified an attempt to divorce jazz from its roots in black culture, to produce a music that 'they' could play. This is not to say that it was all bad—at its best, for instance in the work of Stan Getz, it produced some fine music. But as a school it was sterile, leaving no lasting influences on jazz's subsequent development, and by the early 1960s it had effectively died out.[25]

Hard bop, on the other hand, was to be one of the most influential schools of jazz ever. It began as a reaction primarily against the cool school, but was also powered by a recognition of the dead end that bebop had reached.

Political jazz—from hard bop to the 'new jazz'

Like bebop, hard bop had an explicitly political edge to it. Frank Kofsky argued that:

> Viewed strictly as a **movement among musicians** (which it wasn't), hard bop amounted to a black rebellion against the bleaching tendencies of the cool/West Coast whites. As such, it tended deliberately to lay particular stress on the contemporary forms of urban black music, in the form of blues and gospel.[26]

Art Blakey, one of the founders of and seminal figures in hard bop, made the same point rather differently,

The black musician...his thing is to swing. Well, the only way the Caucasian musician can swing is at the end of a rope. Swinging is our field and we should stay in it.[27]

By the early 1950s bebop found itself in a dead end. With its technical innovations unmatched by any developments in musical forms, it had become increasingly repetitive and derivative of the first generation, many of whom were by then dead or past their prime. Hard bop set out to revitalise bebop by taking its technical develoments and marrying them to more popular forms of black music. Hard bop itself was marked by few technical innovations.What made it different was that it drew from all forms of black American music, in particular gospel and rhythm and blues, and laid a great emphasis on original compositions. It was a music not just explicitly black but proud to be black. And it was to have a profound, if largely unacknowledged, influence on the later rise of soul music.

And it was no accident that it arose in the mid-1950s, as the Civil Rights Movement was beginning in the south, and in the north black pride and aspirations were growing, symbolised by the rise of the Black Muslims. By 1960 there were some 100,000 members of the Muslims in the northern cities, the largest black political movement since the heyday of the National Association for the Advancement of Colored People during World War II. Though few musicians joined them many adopted the Muslim faith as a sign of their alienation from American society.

The rising black movement of the late 1950s and early 1960s increasingly politicised musicians of all generations. Duke Ellington, Count Basie, Coleman Hawkins and Art Blakey among many others all declared their support for the southern struggle. But it was the 'new jazz' musicians of the early 1960s who became the most politically conscious and outspoken, as civil rights gave way to black power. They regularly played benefits for the Student Non-violent Co-ordinating Committee, the Congress for Racial Equality and other civil rights organisations, and gave their compositions increasingly political titles. The first major public showcase for the new music, held in 1964, was billed as 'The October Revolution'. And by 1965 Archie Shepp was arguing that jazz:

...is anti-war; it is opposed to Vietnam; it is for Cuba; it is for the liberation of all people. That is the nature of jazz. That's not far-fetched. Why is that so? Because jazz is a music itself born out of oppression, born out of the enslavement of my people.[28]

Yet within this there was a curious paradox. While the musicians became more explicitly political, their music became increasingly estranged from black audiences. The audience for the new jazz was overwhelmingly white. Think, for instance, of the great live John Coltrane recordings—*Live in Paris*, *Live in Stockholm*, *Live at the Village Vanguard*—not the Harlem Apollo. Even the 'October Revolution' concert was held at a club in New York's West 90s, a predominantly white student/bohemian neighbourhood.

Two processes were at work. The first was inside the new music. The 'new jazz' is harder to define than any other jazz school: what united the musicians who made it was primarily a rejection of what had come before. In striving for more self expression, they moved towards greater complexity, replacing the idea of one single rhythm with poly-rhythms, a pulsing beat which shifted in and out of conventional time, and moving away from the European harmonic structures of keys and chords in favour of a modal system of harmonies. This was in large part inspired by a political rejection of European traditions in favour of African and other traditional music.

Many of the new musicians rejected the very term jazz as a white invention, insisting that what they were playing was simply black music. Some even described the blues as 'slave music' which they had to move beyond. This rejection of the old ways was inspired by a profound revulsion against the devaluation and trivialisation of black culture, as well as being a revolt against the disgusting conditions in which even the highest-paid jazz musicians were forced to work.

At its best—for example in the work of Coltrane, Charles Mingus, Archie Shepp and Albert Ayler—the new jazz produced some of the most moving and profound jazz ever. It is a rich, harsh and exciting music, but one which requires serious concentration. Though the musicians developed in a variety of different directions, one common factor united them—theirs was a serious music to be listened to with respect, it was not dance music. While this attitude propelled them towards greater heights of creativity and inspiration, it also necessarily led them further and further away from a mass audience. The drummer Jerome Cooper summed up their approach:

> *Take B B King. I've worked with him; he's an entertainer, he's supposed to do that. When you go and see him, he has a show. He's an artist, too, but he's a **craftsman**. He's an artist and entertainer. I don't consider myself an entertainer. I consider myself an artist and I do not entertain.*[29]

The second factor was the rise of soul music, not just a dance music but one which, even in its least political forms (Tamla Motown), expressed a new black confidence and determination, and, as the 1960s wore on, increasingly explicit pride and demands: Aretha Franklin's *Respect*, The Impressions' *Move On Up* and *People Get Ready* and of course James Brown's *Say it Loud, I'm Black and I'm Proud*.

Soul and 'popular' music

The struggles waged by blacks in the 1950s and 1960s meant that black music had progressed to a point where all the ideas, frustrations and rages that jazz had expressed instrumentally could now be said out loud. Jazz as protest music was a coded music of attitudes: by the middle 1960s it was possible to go beyond that. And although soul and Tamla quickly found a mass white audience, it always had a proportionally larger black audience. Berry Gordy, Motown's founder, estimated that of a million-selling single 30 percent would be sold to blacks.[30]

The brash confidence and exuberance that the music radiated had an effect irrespective of what the performers—many of whom were very conservative, and concerned simply to build their careers—intended. Martha Reeves, for instance, always denied that *Dancing in the Street* had anything to do with rioting. But the way she denied it showed all too clearly how soul reflected different attitudes and aspirations.

> *Because you are black and it's 1967, a cute teen song gets viewed as some statement. People make you out to be what they think you ought to be. Like I said, I never called anyone to riot. I was calling my ten brothers and sisters to the table. All I wanted was a little gravy. For all of us.*[31]

Few of the people who took to the streets in Watts, Harlem or Newark would have disagreed with those last two sentences. It's important to stress that soul and Tamla were equally authentic expressions of black attitudes, because there was a crucial weakness in the dominant left tradition, which led it to completely misunderstand the importance of youth culture in the 1950s and 1960s. The weakness was the rigid distinction made between 'popular' or 'folk' music (a definition that slipped all too easily into crass nationalism) and 'commercial' music, by definition a bad thing. Here, for instance, is Eric Hobsbawm on rock 'n' roll:

> *It is an awe-inspiring experience to see substantially the same selection of shockers on the automatic gramophones of little Italian towns as in Manchester, and no doubt Wichita, and to reflect that complete freedom of cultural competition would almost certainly put them on those of Moscow and Shanghai....the habitual rock-and-roll fan, unless mentally rather retarded, tends to be between ten and 15 years of age. Probably the universal appeal of the fashion is due to this infantilism. How long the rhythm and blues vogue will last, is another question.*[32]

Roll over, Mick Jagger, and tell Professor Hobsbawm the news.

Even Val Wilmer, one of the most astute jazz writers, bemoaned the fact that in Ghana in 1970 the vast majority of young people wanted to listen to James Brown rather than jazz or 'authentic' Ghanaian music.[33]

Neither rock'n' roll nor soul music fitted Hobsbawm's definition of 'vigorous and resistant folk-music...never swamped by the cultural standards of the upper classes'. Yet in the 1950s and 1960s they became the crucial vehicles for expressing mass alienation from and rebellion against the system, despite being produced by some of the biggest capitalist corporations. They, and not jazz, had become 'a people's music'.

The weakness in Hobsbawm's definition was that it was drawn from a period when essentially all music was produced and heard live, usually by small and geographically limited audiences and when, in the case of jazz, there was a near absolute separation between black and white worlds. The development of urban folk cultures, in America as elsewhere, was a product of relatively short, transitional periods, when a new working class was coming into being. From the 1930s onwards the developments of radio, jukeboxes, television and cheap audio equipment—the mass commoditisation of culture—broke that separation down. (In particular, from the early 1950s onwards, radio and the spread of cheap records opened up a massive white audience for black American music.) As Duncan Hallas argued in a rather different context:

...the question of whether socialist consciousness arises 'spontaneously' amongst workers or is imposed by intellectuals from the 'outside' has absolutely no relevance to modern conditions. It is strictly a non-question because it assumes the existence of a more or less autonomous working-class world outlook into which something is injected. Whether the relatively homogenous working class outlook...was ever so autonomous as has often been supposed may be questioned. In any case it is dead, killed by changing social conditions and above all by the mass media... It is rather ridiculous to argue about whether one should bring ideas from 'outside' to workers who own television sets.[34]

This development is one that has greatly benefitted the working class, by extending cultural horizons and making generally available a far wider range of cultural experiences than before. It follows from this that the idea of a rigid separation between 'the authentic' and 'the commercial' is one that socialists should treat with great suspicion. At worst, it leads to irrelevance in defending as 'real' popular music that almost no one listens to (as the British Communist Party did with the folksong revival in the 1950s, in an attempt to defend 'British' culture against 'creeping Americanisation'). At best it leads to the elitist attitudes which dominate the media studies industries, that all commercially produced mass culture is mindless pap, and that workers, sponge-like, absorb all its reactionary messages when they consume it.[35]

The reality is that really popular mass culture, precisely because it is selling to a mass audience, has to speak to the lives of that audience. As people's lives and experiences change, so popular culture has to change to reflect that. At high points of struggle (as in the 1960s), it reflects that struggle. And while it's true that many aspects of popular culture are laden with ideology, workers interpret those messages in the light of their own experiences, rather than swallowing them wholesale.

Jazz since the 1960s

From the 'new jazz' onwards, jazz went into a decline as other, more dynamic, forms of black music attracted new generations of black musicians. The 'new jazz' itself, influential as Coltrane continued to be, produced very little in the way of a second generation. This was partly because of its isolation from newer forms of black music, and to a lesser extent because many of its founders moved on to academia. Black studies courses, one of the few tangible gains of the 1960s, provided for many of the musicians the most stable jobs they had ever had, and their growth took away from regular playing many musicians.[36]

By the late 1960s there was a return among many jazz musicians to a more approachable dance music, taking in influences from soul and rock music. Miles Davis was once again crucial to this shift, with *Bitches Brew* and *Live-Evil* being credited as beginning the jazz-rock or jazz-funk style which was to flourish in the 1970s and 1980s with bands such as the Crusaders, and those of Bootsy Collins and Maceo Parker. But it was clear that these were black groups drawing on jazz as one influence among many, rather than jazz groups who were taking the music forwards.

The rise of jazz-funk was seen by some simplistic commentators as the musical parallel to the decline of the black movement in the 1970s and 1980s, an apolitical and commercialised music for apolitical times. In fact, at its best it represented a much more interesting process: the convergence of a number of previously separated threads of black American music. Musicians who had begun their working lives in soul bands were looking for forms that allowed them greater freedom, while jazz musicians were looking for ways back to the mainstream black audience; and both were heavily influenced by musicians like Sly Stone and Jimi Hendrix who had begun to weld together blues, soul and rock music in distinctive new ways.

While individual 'new jazz' musicians continued to develop their art, such as Archie Shepp and Ornette Coleman, much of the vitality of jazz over the last 20 years came from the older musicians—Miles Davis, Sonny Rollins and Art Blakey in particular. Yet the fact remains that they were evolving and honing their past styles, rather than making any new breakthroughs. Recent developments in rap and hip-hop have shown that jazz remains an important influence for black musicians to draw on, but also that it is no longer at the leading edge of black music. It remains a vital part of black music, even if today mostly a subsidiary one, but one which develops primarily by going back to its past.

It was no accident that the most interesting development in jazz over the last few years, the growth of black British jazz, drew its inspiration overwhelmingly from hard bop—both a political and a musical inspiration. Hard bop represented for the musicians both a music of black pride and dance music for a mass audience—the last major jazz school to do both.

Jazz flourished, waxed and waned, and has been declining for a number of years as the music on the edge of progress. It is important not to mourn this, or pretend that it's not happened, but to understand why. For understanding the ways in which jazz was rooted in the growth of the black American working class also helps us to understand the most important development in black music in the 1980s—the explosion of urban African music onto the world stage. From Algerian *rai* to South African township *mbaqanga*, the new musics coming out of Africa are products of the creation of African working classes, some of them stretching back 20 or 30 years, others of much more recent vintage.

Like jazz, those musics have developed as syntheses of 'traditional' music with Western influences, both from the many strands of black American music and Western pop music generally. And like jazz too, those musics have shown themselves capable of absorbing many other diverse influences—as in the work of Salif Keita and Youssou N'Dour—and making out of them a music with all the drive and creative power of the best jazz. Similar developments in Latin America, China[37] and elsewhere are likewise signs of the growth and stirrings of new working classes. 'World music' is the reflection and product of the rise of a world working class.

Notes

This article grew out of a talk given at Marxism 92. Particular thanks are due to Teresa O'Donnell and Martin Smith for their help in clarifying my ideas, to Mike Hobart for his thought provoking comments on my arguments, and to everyone who participated in the discussion at the meeting.

1   A similar argument is advanced in Nelson George's controversial *The Death of Rhythm and Blues* (London, 1989) although his book focuses almost entirely on soul and rythm and blues. His basic argument (crudely, that black artists sold their souls to adapt to the tastes of a more lucrative white audience) is questionable, but

the book is one of the most interesting critical evaluations of black music in recent years.

2   I'm only going to discuss jazz in America, both for reasons of space, and also because I'd argue that almost all other 'national' jazz traditions are essentially derived from American jazz (the important exception being South Africa, which requires a separate article to do it justice).

3   L Trotsky, *Literature and Revolution* (London, 1991) pp207-8.

4   L Jones, *Blues People* (New York, 1963) pp7-8 (emphases in original). This is *the* book to read on the social roots of black music, particularly important for his insistence on the diversity of African cultures, a valuable antidote to the essentialist arguments of more recent 'Africanist' writers. For more detailed descriptions of how this black American culture was created, see E Genovese, *Roll, Jordan, Roll* (New York, 1976) and L Levine, *Black Culture and Black Consciousness* (New York, 1977).

5   Think of the music of Cab Calloway, for instance. Is it blues, or jazz, or rhythm and blues? Putting the question like that shows the artificiality of the boundaries.

6   Although there's no space here to develop the argument, it is important to stress that gospel music has had a far greater influence on the development of black American music generally acknowledged in most of the histories.

7   F Newton, *The Jazz Scene* (London, 1963) p43. The book has since been reissued under Hobsbawm's own name (London, 1990). Francis Newton was the pseudonym Hobsbawm used for his writings on jazz. He justified this by arguing that he wanted to keep a separation between his historical work and his jazz writing, but it's probable that the Communist Party's view of jazz as 'decadent' was an equally important reason.

8   My thanks to Jeff Hurford for this point.

9   E Hobsbawm, op cit, p64.

10   J L Collier, *The Making of Jazz: a Comprehensive History* (London, 1981), p78.

11   J Berendt, *The Jazz Book* (London, 1984) p68.

12   For a fuller history of the development of Kansas City music, see R Russells's *Bird Lives!* (London,1976) and *Jazz Style in Kansas City and the Southwest* (California, 1971).

13   The scene in Clint Eastwood's film *Bird,* in which Charlie Parker is driven from the bandstand by a cymbal thrown at him, was, according to Parker, the turning point in his musical development. See *Bird Lives!*, pp84-93.

14   J L Collier, *Benny Goodman and the Swing Era* (London, 1989), p257.

15   Ibid, p87.

16   Ibid, p304.

17   E Hobsbawm, op cit, p85.

18   L Jones, op cit, p177.

19   For contemporary accounts of both the racist attacks and the resistance, see C L R James et al, *Fighting Racism in World War II* (New York, 1980). Roosevelt's order is quoted on p116.

20   F Kofsky, *Black Nationalism and the Revolution in Music* (New York, 1970), p56.

21   R Russell, *Bird Lives!*, op cit, pp257-258.

22   Ibid, p271.

23   N George, op cit, p23.

24   Wyonie Harris, whose frenetic and powerful style was a direct outgrowth of Kansas City swing, is not even mentioned in Collier's 500 page *The Making of Jazz: a Comprehensive History.*

25   This point has aroused a great many controversies in discussions, and it's therefore worth saying something about the role of whites in jazz. I am emphatically not arguing the (patronising if not racist) position that 'only blacks can play jazz'—one of the first records that converted me to jazz was a live concert of Joe Turner and

Buck Clayton backed by the Zagreb Jazz Quartet! Since the 1940s, when it became possible for multi-racial bands to play together in America, every major figure from Parker to Coltrane included at least one white player in a band at one time or another, so clearly they didn't believe it either. What I will argue is that, as jazz is a product of black experiences in America, whites can only properly play it if they have some appreciation of and respect for those experiences and traditions. And the simple truth is that most white incursions into jazz (Paul Whiteman, swing, cool and the endless Dixieland revivals) have been attempts to appropriate the music away from black culture. Only a minority of white musicians (in America, that is— the situation has always been very different elsewhere) have ever attempted to play within the black tradition (learning from, rather than stealing from) which probably explains why the number of great white jazz musicians can be counted on the fingers of one hand.

26   F Kofsky, op cit, p25 (emphasis in original).
27   Quoted in A Taylor, *Notes and Tones* (London, 1983), p249. Blakey, of course, regularly employed white musicians—see note 25 above.
28   Quoted in F Kofsky, op cit, p64.
29   Quoted in V Wilmer, *As Serious as Your Life* (London, 1987), p26.
30   G Hirshey, *Nowhere to Run* (London,1985) p184. Berry Gordy, the incarnation of black capitalism, actually put it the other way around, boasting that 70 percent of sales were to whites.
31   Quoted in ibid, p192.
32   E Hobsbawm, op cit, p73. The last line was sensibly altered in the more recent edition.
33   V Wilmer, *Mama Said There'd Be Days Like This* (London, 1989), pp199-200.
34   D Hallas, 'Towards a Revolutionary Socialist Party' in Cliff, Harman, Hallas and Trotsky, *Party and Class* (London, no date), p20.
35   P T Barnum was wrong: you can go broke underestimating an audience's intelligence, as the producers and cast of *Eldorado* recently discovered.
36   See V Wilmer, *As Serious...*, op cit, pp241-245.
37   For an interesting account of Chinese syntheses of rock'n'roll, pop music and traditional Chinese music, see 'Rock and roll on the new Long March' by T Brace and P Friedlander, in R Garofalo (ed), *Rockin' the Boat* (Boston, 1992).

Revolution and the challenge of labour

A review of Chris Wrigley (ed), **Challenges of Labour: Central and Western Europe 1917-1920** (Routledge, 1993) £40

DONNY GLUCKSTEIN

History, unlike time, does not advance at an even pace. There are moments when changes that in normal circumstances take decades to occur happen within the space of months or weeks. The humdrum pattern of daily existence is disrupted. Mighty institutions that seemed fixed and immovable can crumble into dust overnight—1789, 1848 and Eastern Europe recently were such moments. Such events create the possibility, for millions of people who often feel powerless to shape their lives, to discover hope and a sense of mass power.

The period 1917-20 is especially significant in this regard. It saw the collapse of an old order and the struggle for birth of a new one. A new book, *Challenges of Labour, Central and Western Europe 1917-1920*, brings together a series of articles on all aspects of this crucial period, a time of mass struggles following the 1917 Russian Revolution.

The question of revolutionary potential

This book is made up of the writings of 13 leading academics from a range of countries. It is not written from a revolutionary socialist point of view. Yet, in spite of this, the revolutionary potential of the period following the 1914-18 war shines through. Indeed, there is a flat contradiction between the commentary some of the writers make about events and the facts they themselves describe.

Let us first look at the commentaries. Dick Geary's article on 'Revolutionary Berlin' argues that those who believed there could be a 'new socialist order...are given little credence by most serious historians,'[1] because 'the prospects of socialist revolution were always remote...'[2] There is an article by Piero Melograni which says that during the so called 'Two Red Years' in Italy (1919-20) 'the revolutionary movement was not very strong.'[3] Another Italian suggests that in Turin—the most militant area—there was not even a working class 'as understood by first the Socialist, then the Communist, agitators of the period'![4] Elsewhere we are told that 'there does not appear to have been a potentially revolutionary situation in Britain'.[5]

Charles Wrigley, the editor, summarises the message. Far from representing an advance:

> *The First World War and its aftermath shattered many illusions of the European left. In spite of the upheavals of such a major war, the capitalist system of the advanced industrial nations did not collapse nor did the working people of those nations rise up and 'follow Russia'... Instead many divisions and contradictions within socialism and the labour movements... now became stark and contributed to the undermining of such opportunities as the left had in 1919-1920.*[6]

Given the book's perspective it is strange to read in these same pages of the enormous scale, breadth and intensity of class struggle. First Germany:

> *In the first ten days of November 1918 the revolution spread the length and breadth of Germany. In Munich, for example, the Wittelsbach monarchy was replaced by armed groups of workers and soldiers... There and elsewhere the old order bowed before the demands of armed workers' and soldiers' councils with little or no resistance.*[7]

In Budapest 'proletarian dictatorship was established peacefully and without resistance.' Vienna, the capital of the Austro-Hungarian Empire, the second largest state in Europe, was rocked by a series of mass strikes which:

> *contributed most to the undermining and removal of the old Austrian authoritarian regime...[and] not only determined the course of the Austrian revolution but also brought to working people in the new state a perceptible improvement in their democratic, social and political rights and scope for effective action.*[8]

Now, it could be objected that an apparent breakdown of these regimes only occurred as a result of disappointment and defeat in the First World War. It is true that the victor powers, France, Britain and Italy, did not witness armed overthrow of governments. But this does not mean that the potential was lacking for just such an event. Once again the book presents excellent evidence to contradict its own perspective.

In May-June 1919, writes Roger Magraw, Paris was gripped by a 'quasi-insurrectionary' strike of metal workers which 'set the tone for post-war labour politics'.[9] This was in spite of the relatively better conditions of the victorious French government. In April they had, after all, 'rushed through the Eight-Hour Day Act in the hope of heading off worker unrest—a hope rudely dashed by events of the following weeks.'[10] Nonetheless militants 'found a receptive audience for denunciation of Allied intervention in Russia and in April 100,000 Parisian workers had marched to protest at the acquittal of [the socialist leader] Jaures's assassin.' On May Day 1919 demonstrations turned into 'massive confrontations with police and troops in which 600 workers were arrested and hundreds, mainly building workers and metal workers, were injured—two fatally.'[11] Thus 'fear of revolution was an insistent theme of the entire post-war period.'[12]

At Fiat in Italy, too, attempts to appease worker discontent had an impact contrary to that intended:

> *Thus, in a situation in which everyone was expecting substantial improvements, the claims of one category boosted those of another in an upward spiral that worried the management all the more as it recognised the pointlessness of further economic concessions. There was no longer any guarantee that satisfaction of demands would reduce the risk of further disputes. In fact the opposite might happen and the workers become more demanding as long as the company proved conciliatory.*[13]

John Foster's article on the Clyde quotes from Prime Minister Lloyd George's evaluation of the period:

> *The Russian Revolution lit up the skies with a lurid flash of hope for all who were dissatisfied with the existing order of things... In Russia, they pointed out, the workmen formed a separate authority to co-ordinate with the government... Why not in Britain? This was the question asked in every workshop and at every street corner.*[14]

Foster goes on to argue that 'Clydeside was able to relate in a particularly direct fashion to models of social change provided by the Bolshevik revolution.'[15]

Class and revolution

In constructing the argument that socialist revolution was not on the agenda (and by extension is impossible now), a common device is to suggest that the potential forces are just too weak. The masses are portrayed as splintered into different and competing groups. Today the divisions are often seen as women versus men, blue collar versus white collar, soldiers versus workers, and—in economically backward countries—country people versus townsfolk.

This suits the analysis presented in *Challenges of Labour*, but despite the intentions of most of the contributors, the book explodes the myth and does so very effectively. Although there was supposed to be no 'class' in Turin, the links between different groupings were established by their very actions. The 'Two Red Years' at Fiat actually began with a strike by white collar workers, a large percentage of whom were women. Meetings were always chaired by women—the 'Signorine'. When management tried to split the labour force by offering male manual workers pay rises during the strike they refused to accept until the white collar workers had won. On the strength of this movement the technical grades immediately came forward with their own set of demands.

In Paris the 100,000 women working in the weapons factories were given the patronising nickname 'munitionnettes' by the press. But there is evidence of the way they began to get organised and link up not only with industrial agitation around pay and conditions, but with anti-war activities. In 1917 they formed one third of the audience at strike rallies and chanted for the return of 'their men' from the army. Seamstresses forced a cut in the working week, and milliners won double pay while munitions workers demanded pay rises, denounced brutal foremen and demanded extra holidays for those with menfolk on leave from the army.[16] Furthermore, in France:

> *no huge gulf emerged between* [white collar] *employees and blue collar workers... Indeed after 1920 it was precisely public service employees who became the backbone of a* [trade union movement] *which was desperately weak in private industry.*[17]

The workers' movement was involved in community protests over food prices, public amenities, sewage, educational and health provision. A 50,000 strong tenants association organised direct action squads against evictions, and began the tradition which in the 1930s made this area 'the notorious "red belt".'[18]

Hostility between towns and a supposedly reactionary countryside has often been cited as a reason for the impossibility of socialist revolution in backward economies. However, even ignoring the example of Russia in 1917, Hungary showed the potential:

> The revolution triumphed in Budapest on 31 October 1918. From that time on right up to mid-November a real peasant revolt swept across the country. The first riots were again started by the starving local population, just as in the summers of 1917 and 1918, but they were soon joined in early November by the masses of armed soldiers coming home from the fronts.[19]

Given the ethnic divisions in Eastern Europe and the current arguments about the inevitability of nationalist conflicts, it is interesting to read that:

> The early November mass riots had no significant nationality features. Hungarian peasants attacked their mainly Hungarian landlords and village notaries just as fiercely as their fellows belonging to other nationalities did, and non-Hungarian landlords and their estates were to face a fate similar to that of the Hungarian ones in the neighbourhood. In regions with a mixed population the peasants belonging to different nationalities often combined forces. The peasantry of the national minorities expressed in November 1918 no national goals and was the object of, rather than the active party in, the separatist aspirations and movements.[20]

Finally, even in Britain, the country least damaged by the war, barriers between different groups began to fall away. Not only did trade unionism expand amongst ordinary workers, there were even serious efforts made to organise in the police force and army. Amongst the police this led to strikes, while in the army the Soldiers', Sailors' and Airmen's Union (SSAU) was formed. The formation of such a body contributed to a more rapid demobilisation of soldiers. In spite of this mutinies broke out. While the one in Calais is well known, mutinies in Russia and in Punjab also occurred. These mutinies were only put down when the dissidents' camps were surrounded by brigades armed with machine guns. The government served out exemplary 'justice' to deter others from the same course:

> In Russia, over a period of six months, 87 men were court-martialled, with 13 receiving death sentences (later commuted). Of those men tried in the Punjab, 14 received death sentences…James Daly…was executed.[21]

If there were potential and real links between mass actions of apparently diverse groups, then the argument against the possibility of a unified revolutionary challenge is weakened. So another argument must be deployed. This is to point out that the numbers involved in a con-

scious revolutionary movement were small. In one sense this argument is
valid, but not in the way the authors of *Challenges of Labour* intend. As
will be shown later, the absence of organised revolutionaries was a
crucial problem. However, this is not the point that the authors seek to
make. Rather, they split up mass activities into separate compartments
along the lines of revolutionary, labourist and constitutional action to
show that pure, consciously revolutionary action was minimal.

However, the actual events again cry out against this analysis. We
read that the Kiel mutiny that began the German Revolution of
November 1918 was started by sailors,

> *after years cooped up in port with lousy rations and no sympathy from their
> officers... Not much of a revolution, many have commented: the sailors had
> immediate grievances but little desire to change the political world. They
> were concerned with rations, the release of their friends and above all not to
> have to fight.*[22]

And yet, as the book grudgingly points out: 'In themselves demands
for peace and the freeing of political prisoners were *not devoid* of political consequences...'[my emphasis].[23] This is a fantastic understatement.
No revolution has ever begun in a fully conscious way. That of 1789
began when a parliament refused to disband. The 1905 Russian revolution began with a march to humbly beseech the Tsar to grant reforms,
and 1917 began when women demanded bread. In Germany the sailors'
mutiny against the state, whose very basis consists of the exclusive
control of physical force, is a highly political act with dire consequences
should it fail. The sailors knew of the executions of previous mutineers.
That was why the November revolution swept Germany within the space
of ten days. It was the sailors of Kiel rushing as quickly as they could all
over the country that spread the revolution and they did so consciously—
their lives were at stake if they failed! This was indeed 'not devoid of
political consequences'.

If it is ridiculous to try and put up barriers between economics and
politics in defeated countries, the strategy seems more plausible in victor
countries. Articles on Britain and France make a sharp distinction
between conscious revolutionary organisations—which were small and
weak—and the general labour movement which, it is pointed out, was
interested in bread and butter issues. John Foster's article on the Clyde is
effective in demolishing the arguments of right wing historians like Iain
McLean who, in *The Legend of Red Clydeside*, pretends that nothing significant happened at all. Unfortunately Foster falls into the trap of
separating revolutionary politics and economics by arguing, in semi-
nationalist fashion, that there was something specially radical about the
Scottish labour movement which set it off from backward England.

Clydeside was unique in a number of ways, in particular in possessing an impressive revolutionary voice in the group around John Maclean. But the greatest potential for shaking the system lay with the miners' struggle on a national scale.

Another article on Britain achieves the same division of economics and politics by a different route. After dealing with the *Jolly George* incident and near general strike which were against British military intervention against Russia, Chris Wrigley turns to the supposedly separate area of economic conflict. He is aware of the 'sheer number' of strikes in Britain. In 1920 there were 1,607 strikes involving 1,932,000 people and costing 26,568,000 days, but decides, 'Whether such strikes presaged a major threat to the existing social order is another matter.'[24] In France we are told in identical terms that 'there was little politicised or subversive unrest... Labour unrest was another matter.'[25]

'Another matter'? Such an approach, which sees the revolutionary movement as distinct from mass strike action for economic ends, is strongly reminiscent of the right wing German social democrats Rosa Luxemburg criticised after 1905 in her pamphlet on *The Mass Strike*. In the section on 'The Interaction of the Political and the Economic Struggle' she wrote:

> *Instead of the rigid and hollow scheme of an arid political action carried out by the decision of the highest committees...we see a bit of pulsating life of flesh and blood, which cannot be cut out of the large frame of the revolution but is connected with all parts of the revolution by a thousand veins... Political and economic strikes, mass strikes and partial strikes, demonstrative strikes and fighting strikes, general strikes of individual branches of industry and general strikes in individual towns, peaceful wage struggles and street massacres, barricade fighting—all these run through one another, run side by side, cross one another, flow in and over one another...*[26]

Europe in 1917-20 saw all of the phenomena Luxemburg described. The fact that they did not culminate in successful socialist revolutions is not due so much to an unbridgeable gap between the struggle for pay and the struggle for power. It was the lack of a conscious socialist force trying to develop the connections, an organisation which could convince large numbers that the only long term solution to economic problems was the overthrow of capitalism, just as the struggle for the overthrow of capitalism grew out of the immediate struggles in the factories, offices and mines. But before dealing with this it is necessary to look at the alternative viewpoint put in *Challenges of Labour*.

The ruling class response

The great question hanging over the European class struggles of 1917-20 is why there was no successful socialist revolution outside of Russia. *Challenges of Labour* claims to explain this in its second half which 'is made up of essays on major aspects of the resurgence of the old order...'[27] However, it is here that the book is most disappointing. The idea of a 'resurgence of the old order' implies new methods, great political skills and sophistication in heading off unprecedented dangers, and so on. Yet we will search in vain for major evidence of such things.

In Hungary 'the fall of the council republic was primarily due to international power relations...'[28] It was no cunning strategy but 'the superior power of the external armies [that broke] the resistance of the still half-organised red army and...proletarian dictatorship...'[29] In France we read that, 'for a traditional threat, the state used traditional repression'.[30] Its key innovation was to organise scabbing including 'patriotic groups, the more conservative veterans' organisations, and women's voluntary nursing and aid associations...'[31] None of this is very startling. The historian of Italy tells us no more than that 'the revolution had not come [as] it had not been wanted.'[32] For Britain we read, 'With a mixture of concession and firmness the British propertied classes came through the turmoil of the immediate post-war years with their privileges and wealth mostly intact.'[33]

Only in Germany is a specifically new strategy for heading off revolution presented: the rapid demobilisation of the army. This supposedly allowed for the dispersing of the discontented radical soldiers and retention of a reactionary elite for use in the near civil war that swept Germany afterwards. Even here the argument is not fully convincing.[34]

The break up of the army in Germany, like the forced acceleration of demobilisation in Britain and elsewhere, was not the result of skilful government planning. It was imposed on the governments by the pressure of the discontented soldiers themselves. It is difficult to imagine the German High Command rejoicing in the fact that:

> in the six weeks between the conclusion of the Armistice treaty and Christmas 1918 throughout the country about 5 million German soldiers left military service, and in January 1919 yet another 2 million followed them. The chairman of the German Armistice Commission, Matthias Erzberger, stated in a speech on 15 January 1919, 'The German Army has vanished.'[35]

In fact, during the war governments found that the quickest and surest means of achieving obedience and crushing opposition had been to conscript militant workers. The British government had tried to do this with the unofficial shop stewards' movement in Sheffield and been compelled to back off by mass strike action. It was regularly used in Italy where up to one third of factory workers were under military discipline.

Mass demobilisation brought about by mass mutiny, as in the German case, is not a convincing reason for the failure of the revolutionary movement—it was one of its successes. The demobbed soldiers could have been welded into a revolutionary force *if* the will to organise such a force had been present on a large enough scale. It was not, and that was the key issue in Germany, as elsewhere.

The absence of a revolutionary party

The weakness of the book's explanation for the failure of the revolutionary wave lies in this final point. Capitalism's strength did not save it from destruction. If, as has been shown above, the *potential* for a socialist overthrow of society was there and yet the working class failed to realise that potential, then the problem must have been a subjective one. It was the lack of mass revolutionary parties arguing within the class that really explains the outcome of the 1917-20 period.

The writers in *Challenges of Labour* point all too easily to the weakness of the organised revolutionary forces. In Germany the Communist Party was not founded till weeks *after* the outbreak of revolution in November 1918. The Austrian Communist Party was founded just one week before the overthrow of the Hapsburgs and 'eked out a shadowy existence until spring 1919'.[36] In France it was not until December 1920 that revolutionaries founded a distinct party. The Italian Communist Party was actually founded in 1921, after the revolutionary wave had passed, and Britain was just as late.

Perhaps the most unusual party was that of the Hungarian Communists, founded on 24 November 1918 and in power on 21 March 1919. This sudden rise to influence was of little use, since the lack of experience led to elementary yet disastrous mistakes. Facing a peasantry who were a major force the Soviet government should have distributed the big estates amongst them. This 'could have won them over to the revolution's side, even though they held the traditional order and hierarchy of the village to be natural'.[37] Without this move the regime was easily isolated and defeated from without.

The weakness of revolutionary organisation is taken as evidence of lack of radicalism in the working class in general. However, most of the writers in *Challenges of Labour* want to avoid stress on the subjective element, since that would suggest a revolutionary potential for the working class. The nearest most of them get to the issue is to complain about 'divisions of the Left'.[38] Once again the evidence clashes with the interpretation. The problem of subjective weaknesses in the working class is most clearly demonstrated by comparing the revolutionaries with reformist Social Democrats and union officials in various countries.

Hans Hautmann, writing on Vienna, makes the role of the latter wonderfully clear:

> When [during January 1919] *the first workers' councils began to form spontaneously in a series of strike-bound works, the Social Democratic Party took by the horns the bull it could no longer avoid and, of its own accord, called upon the workers to erect workers' councils everywhere. The purpose behind this, to win back its lost control over the masses and to regain its hold over the movement, was fulfilled...the Social Democratic Party executive succeeded in obtaining a resolution of the Viennese Workers' Council to end the strike. In spite of the fierce resistance of many workers the action began to crumble away on 21 January. On 24 January the great general strike, which had brought the system of rule in Austria to the very edge of the abyss, was at an end.*[39]

In France, Merrheim, the leader of the metal workers' union (FM), played a key role. He helped bring about a sell out of the Paris metal workers' strike in the summer of 1919 because he:

> *hoped to create a large, disciplined industrial union capable of bargaining with the patronat* [bosses]... *'Those who believe that one can consume more and produce less deceive the working masses and prepare them for a future of unspeakable suffering.' He refused to be 'dragged along by the unorganised masses, by the unchained crowd...'*[40]

New realism was as much a dead end then as now. Instead of creating a 'large, disciplined industrial union capable of bargaining', Merrheim's sell out left workers weak in the face of declining military orders and bosses who were out to sack prominent activists. Soon thousands were laid off by the likes of Citroen and Renault while 'unionisation levels collapsed dramatically in the Parisian engineering sector...'[41]

In Britain, too, trade union leaders are described as:

> *bulwarks against a breakdown of order in industry. Thus Sir Robert Horne (Minister of Labour) observed that 'the government could not hope to win through present and future labour battles unless they had the support of the trade union executives' and Bonar Law commented that 'the trade union organisation was the only thing between us and anarchy'.*[42]

The Labour Party played its role, with its leader, Henderson, declaring: 'The problem was to restore popular confidence in representative [parliamentary] institutions and to guide the mass movement along the path of constitutional change.'[43] As in France, there was little gratitude for these sterling efforts on behalf of the ruling class. Henderson, who had gone to Russia during 1917 to try to bolster the reformists against the Bolsheviks, found himself 'damned as one who had "hobnobbed" with Lenin and Trotsky when there. This was a remarkable smear given that Henderson had not met them...'[44]

The situation in Italy was that the Socialist Party 'made a substantial contribution to the preserving of the status quo. The revolutionary potential of the party was paralysed and consumed uselessly.'[45]

It becomes clear that to blame divisions on the left for workers' failure is simplistic. If there had been a division much earlier and a credible revolutionary alternative to reformism established, then the Social Democrats and union officials could have been challenged for leadership of the mass movement.

One writer at least recognises that the subjective factor is an issue. This is Dick Geary in his piece on Berlin. He too wants to write off the potential for socialist revolution, but he has a problem. Firstly, in Germany the reality of revolution was more than apparent. Thus in November 1918 the country was covered by a network of workers' and soldiers' councils. In 1919 a Soviet republic was declared in Bavaria, with numerous risings in places like Hamburg and Bremen occurring. Between 1919 and 1923 there was an almost uninterrupted series of general strikes, coups and counter-coups. Secondly, it was the reformist leaders from within the labour movement who were central in preventing the revolution leading to workers' power. It is just not possible to overlook the fact that the Social Democrats *were the government.* The result was the murder of revolutionaries like Liebknecht and Luxemburg, together with the crushing of risings all over the country. This was organised by the Social Democrat Noske and his Freikorps troops.

Geary solves the problem by suggesting that, rather than failing to fulfil their potential, the Social Democrats more or less represented the working class and so their actions corresponded to the will of significant numbers of workers. Therefore, to describe the sending of troops and Freikorps 'not only against communist insurrections but also against striking metalworkers and miners...as a simple "betrayal" of the German working class...is however, more than a little misleading.'[46] Why? 'The fact that the SPD continued to enjoy the support of a sizeable proportion of the German working class alone is sufficient to indicate the problematical nature of any such claim.'[47]

This will not do, and Geary himself is clearly uncomfortable with this argument. The fact is that the reformist leaders who worked hand in glove with the remnants of the Kaiser's High Command were not in the same position as their rank and file supporters. They had risen on the back of workers' struggle against a repressive government and employing class because they promised to bring a better society and put an end to the sufferings of capitalism. They claimed to *lead* this fight. They *did* betray the class by not only failing to lead but actively collaborating with the capitalists. As Geary says:

> *the fact that Ebert and his colleagues acquiesced in the destruction of the German Left with apparently no bad conscience and did so moreover in collusion with right-wing bodies such as the army High Command and the Freikorps makes one think that the above does not constitute the whole story.*[48]

He does now get to the nub of the issue.

> *In a sense the leadership* [of the Social Democrats] *and for that matter of the Free Trade Unions was concerned with precisely the same issue as the officer corps, namely survival. It wanted to protect its interests.*[49]

This was betrayal on a grand scale of the class that put it into a position of influence.

Challenges of Labour is an important survey of a crucial period in working class history. It fails politically and historically because it tries to squeeze events of a revolutionary character into a reformist interpretation which is both inappropriate for that time and has been shown to be a flawed and dead end approach today. The academics who produced it have extensive knowledge of their subject in a dry academic sense, yet most show a lack of understanding as to what a revolution is about. It is easy to look back and say that since revolution did not spread successfully outside Russia this proves no other outcome was possible. But history is not just about what was, but about what could have been. This is not a matter of wishful thinking, of wanting reality to be different, but of recognising that people make choices that matter, that 'man makes history, but not in circumstances of his own choosing', as Marx put it.

In the period 1917-20 workers had a unique power and influence. The way they chose to use these was decisive for the future. Tragically the choices they made were dominated by reformist organisations that wished to see capitalism preserved. The failure to take power would lead to the rise of a semi-fascist dictatorship in Hungary and full fascism in Italy, Germany and Austria. There is no other period so rich in lessons for revolutionary socialists, and so the writers of *Challenges of Labour* have, in spite of their best efforts, created a valuable and interesting book.

Notes

1   D Geary, 'Revolutionary Berlin', in C Wrigley (ed), *Challenges of Labour: Central and Western Europe 1917-1920* (Routledge, 1993), p39.
2   Ibid, p47.
3   P Melograni, 'Lenin, Italy and Fairytales', in C Wrigley (ed), op cit, p229.
4   G Berta, 'The Interregnum: Turin, Fiat and Industrial Conflict between War and Fascism', in C Wrigley (ed), op cit, p109.
5   C Wrigley, 'The State and Challenge of Labour in Britain 1917-1920', in C Wrigley (ed), op cit, p262.
6   Ibid, p289.
7   D Geary, op cit, p36.
8   H Hautmann, 'Vienna: a City in the Years of Radical Change 1917-1920', in C Wrigley (ed), op cit, p103.
9   R Magrew, 'Paris 1917-1920: Labour Protest and Popular Politics', in C Wrigley (ed), op cit, p136.
10   Ibid, pp136-137.
11   Ibid, p137.
12   J Horne, 'The State and the Challenge of Labour in France 1917-1920', in C Wrigley (ed), op cit, p248.
13   G Berta, op cit, p114.
14   J Foster, 'Working Class Mobilisation on the Clyde 1917-1920', in C Wrigley (ed), op cit, p163.
15   Ibid, p159.
16   R Magrew, op cit, p132.
17   Ibid, p144.
18   Ibid, p140.
19   I Romsics, 'The Hungarian Peasantry and the Revolutions of 1918-19', in C Wrigley (ed), op cit, p202.
20   Ibid, pp202-203
21   C Wrigley, op cit, p269.
22   D Geary, op cit, p37.
23   Ibid, p37.
24   C Wrigley, op cit, p271.
25   J Horne, op cit, p249.
26   R Luxemburg, *Rosa Luxemburg Speaks* (New York, 1970), pp181-182.
27   C Wrigley, op cit, p1.
28   Z Nagg, 'Budapest and the Revolutions of 1918 and 1919', in C Wrigley (ed), op cit, p83.
29   Ibid, p83.
30   J Horne, op cit, p253.
31   Ibid, p254.
32   P Melograni, op cit, p254.
33   C Wrigley, op cit, p283.
34   For details see C Harman, *Germany: The Lost Revolution* (London, 1982).
35   W Wette, 'Demobilisation in Germany 1918-19, the Gradual Erosion of the Powers of the Soldiers' Councils', in C Wrigley, op cit, p183.
36   H Hautmann, op cit, p97.
37   I Romsics, op cit, p207.
38   D Geary, op cit, p47, and C Wrigley, op cit, p295.
39   H Hautmann, op cit, p94.
40   R Magrew, op cit, p137.
41   Ibid, p139.
42   C Wrigley, op cit, p275.

43   Ibid, p278.
44   Ibid, p279.
45   P Melograni, op cit, p236.
46   D Geary, op cit, p41.
47   Ibid, p41.
48   Ibid, p42.
49   Ibid, p42.

Bookwatch: the Labour Party in decline

CHARLIE KIMBER

There is a conviction in some quarters that the Tories will almost inevitably win the next election. This in part reflects the deep seated pessimism of many on the left. They believe that workers are so dulled by right wing ideas that they will never fight and are always prey to the siren calls of the media. On the surface such pessimism seems incredible. Labour is consistently 15 to 20 percent ahead of the Tories in opinion polls. John Major's government is the most unpopular since records began and his personal popularity has sunk to coincide with the rate of VAT—17.5 percent.

But the belief that Labour could easily lose the next election is also rooted in some past experience. Labour lost in 1992 despite being 20 percent ahead in the polls at the time of the Trafalgar Square poll tax riot and being 16 percent in front during the ambulance workers' dispute in 1989-90. So many Labour Party members, on the left as well as the right, believe that drastic changes are required in order to avoid a repeat performance.

Four recently published books provide a useful background to Labour's present crisis. They also provide a history of how Labour reacted to the many opportunities available to socialists in the 1980s—the steel strike, the health workers' dispute, the poll tax rebellion, the ambulance workers' dispute, the movement against nuclear weapons and the Gulf War.

One of the strengths of Richard Heffernan and Mike Marqusee's book *Defeat from the Jaws of Victory* is that it reminds us that those who now wish to preside over 'modernisation' are the same figures who ran the party during the run up to defeat in 1992. Those who have caused the wreckage claim to be the only ones who can carry out reconstruction. And some, like John Smith, have been in the leadership during many years of reverse for Labour.

Smith served as secretary for trade from 1978 to 1979 in the last Labour government. He was part of that administration which did so much to embitter workers against Labour as it doubled unemployment and slashed living standards. Smith was always on the party's right wing. He joined the Solidarity group when it was formed in 1980 after the defection by the Gang of Four to found the SDP. It was designed to repel the left and ensure Labour remained true to pro-Washington, right wing, pro-EC policies. But although he lined up with Solidarity, Smith remained aloof from much of the inner party controversy of the 1980s. Heffernan and Marqusee note:

> *He rarely if ever made any direct attacks on the left. Unlike the 'soft left', he did not have to. Nobody doubted where Smith, an old-style right-winger sponsored by the GMB, stood on the witch-hunt, unilateralism, the Gulf War or reselection.*[1]

His reward was a central place in the 1983 election effort. He was a member of the campaign committee and starred alongside Michael Foot, Neil Kinnock, Peter Shore and others in the TV election broadcasts. Smith's biographers will not be able to claim that his media efforts brought much success. Labour took just 28.3 percent of the vote, its lowest share since 1918. Foot went, but Smith prospered. In 1985 he took over the important trade and industry team and once again was at the leading edge of the 1987 campaign. Again he was in the middle of defeat as Labour lost despite being well ahead in the polls during the 1984-5 miners' strike.

As so frequently with the Labour right, responsibility for utter failure seemed a passport to progress. Smith was honoured to be joint campaign manager for the Kinnock-Hattersley dream ticket when it re-applied for the top positions in 1988. This time, dealing only with opponents inside the party and to the left, he was on the winning side. His years of loyalty to the leadership which drove Labour rightwards meant he was well placed to succeed Hattersley as shadow chancellor in 1989 and then to replace Kinnock last year.

Heffernan and Marqusee also give powerful evidence that the reaction to the latest election loss is very similar to what occurred in 1983 and 1987. The 1983 defeat sent shockwaves through the party. Labour had come third or worst in almost 300 constituencies. Although the national executive held no formal post mortem, right wing MPs and a supporting crew of academic pundits rushed to denounce the left and all its works for the disaster. Shadow cabinet minister Gerald Kaufman denounced the manifesto as 'the longest suicide note in history'.[2] It had, he said, frightened voters into the arms of the Tories. Intellectual support came from Eric Hobsbawm who blamed the left for 'engaging in a civil war rather than fighting the right'.[3] The solution offered by Labour's leaders was a long and thorough process of 'realignment'.

At first the changes seemed quite small. Neil Kinnock's victory in the leadership race was seen as a victory for the centre left and a defeat for the right wing. When Kinnock wrote about 'my socialism' for the *New Statesman* he quoted Marx, Engels, Trotsky and Gramsci.[4] He used the word 'socialism' 39 times. But preparations were already being made for a massive shift in policy. Kinnock could not move too swiftly. The year long miners' strike prevented an immediate move to ditch socialist principles and rhetoric. But he did show his intention by spurning any real solidarity with the strike and tearing into the leaders of Liverpool council who had for a time defied the Tories.

What signalled real change was a further election defeat in 1987. The party rank and file was fully demoralised and there was no miners' strike to prevent the drift rightwards. Now MPs and union leaders demanded a further fundamental shift in policies and presentation. Bryan Gould argued, 'We need to develop radical policies which are not only true to our socialist values but also appeal to the self-interest of those whose votes we need.'[5] Gould argued that the crucial voters were those who were relatively comfortably off. They would only be attracted if Labour embraced the 'popular capitalism' of the Tories. 'The idea of owning shares is catching on,' he insisted, 'and as socialists we should support it as one means of taking power from the few and spreading it more widely.'[6]

Gould's argument was echoed by many others including Nigel Williamson, the editor of Labour's magazine *New Socialist*. He pleaded that, 'Labour needs to attract votes from the better off majority if it is to have a real chance of power.' This required Labour to be 'the party of progress, a modern party which promises a better tomorrow and not merely a better yesterday'.[7] Backing up all this rhetoric were very old fashioned demands for a purge of the left. Party treasurer and seafarers' union leader Sam McCluskie urged the party to change its rules to block the 'hijack of constituency parties by factions unrepresentative of the broad mass of Labour supporters.' He also wanted Labour councils to 'stop espousing the cause of minority interests'.[8]

So there is nothing new in the horrified reaction to the latest election defeat and the frenzied demands to shift policy even further to the right. As Martin Smith says:

> *The policy and organisational changes undertaken by Neil Kinnock are not completely new but a continuation of a process initiated by Gaitskell. All Labour leaders since the 1950s, except Michael Foot, have attempted to modernise the party by identifying it as a national social democratic party. The attempt to change policy started long before the arrival of Mrs Thatcher.* [9]

After Labour's third defeat of a decade in 1959, Gaitskell tried to repudiate completely the image of Labour as a 'party devoted to nationalisation' by removing Clause 4 of the party's constitution. He wanted to drop all mention of class conflict and project Labour as a British party rather than one reflecting class organisation and class feeling.

Harold Wilson continued the process. He gradually removed much of Labour's commitment to public ownership and sheltered behind 'modern' phrases like the 'white heat of the technological revolution'. The climax of this modernisation strategy was the white paper *In Place of Strife* which was an attempt to shackle the unions with laws, courts and fines. Class was out and the 'national interest' (the bosses' interest) was in.

This long history emphasises how jaded and weary the smart phrases about 'modernising' are. Far from charting a new course, David Blunkett and Tony Blair are plodding down a path that has already been tried repeatedly. The history also shows that Labour's problems are both deep and long term. For quite simply all the decades of 'modernising' have not worked, even in the terms defined by the Labour leaders. If what matters is gaining office then 'modernising' is a crushing failure. Labour has managed to lose four elections in a row at a time when there is immense bitterness and frustration at the Tories and also to alienate many of its traditional supporters. In 1992,

> *Exit polls indicated that Labour underperformed among three crucial groups: older women, young men and, most telling of all, its own 'core vote'. Labour won a smaller proportion of the votes of the unemployed than in 1987. It also lost support among council tenants and people on low incomes... It was part of a longer term trend. Since 1966 Labour has gained 4 percent among managerial groups but lost 5 percent among clerical workers, 15 percent among unskilled manual workers and 18 percent among skilled workers.* [12]

How can this be explained? The basic truth is that in the end Labour's electoral support depends on the radicalism generated by workers' struggles. But the whole history of Labour in the 1980s and 1990s is a twofold attempt both to prevent struggles taking place or, if that were not possible, to distance the party from those who were fighting back.

Every great battle finds an echo in the Labour Party because of its links to the trade unions. But Labour's leaders have done their best to shun the workers' action which could have brought down Thatcher much earlier and then scuppered Major. Neil Kinnock launched vicious attacks on the miners' pickets during the Great Strike of 1984-85. He denounced people who could not or would not pay the poll tax. He refused to call for solidarity action with the ambulance workers' dispute in 1989. The change from Kinnock to Smith made no difference. Smith threw away the huge public feeling over the pit closure programme in October 1992. He set his face against the mood for widespread industrial action to force the government to drop its plans—action which if it had happened could have forced Major out and seen Smith in Downing Street.

At the same time as shunning struggle, Labour's policies were shifted ever closer to the Tories'. Often this took an immense internal battle to fundamentally change the party's official positions. It is easy to forget just how much Labour's conference and policy statements have changed. At the 1980 conference delegates had a real chance to debate. Shadow cabinet ministers were forced to wait their turn to speak. Now delegates are little more than observers, presented with policy statements which cannot be amended and treated to lengthy orations from a series of leadership figures.

In 1980 the main economic resolution, moved by the far from revolutionary David Basnett, leader of the GMB, demanded restrictions on the flight of capital, an 'extension of public ownership with industrial democracy', 'reflation of public service spending', 'a substantial cut in arms spending', a 'wealth tax', a 35 hour week without loss of pay and recognition that 'Britain's social and economic problems can only be resolved by socialist planning'.[11] It was passed overwhelmingly with the leadership's support.

By 1992 the party's manifesto had not a single mention of socialism—for the first time in its history. Campaign chief Jack Cunningham could urge, 'the Tories are already planning a rough, dirty election... our credibility is going to be the key issue. We shouldn't promise what we can't deliver, we shouldn't raise hopes, we shouldn't build up people's expectations only to dash them.'[12] In 1983 the constituency section elected seven left wingers to the executive. In 1992 it elected one. At the 1993 conference that lone figure, Tony Benn, saw his vote drop by a third and he was booted off. The constituencies returned 'safe' figures like Blair and Harriet Harman, all from the shadow cabinet.

For some writers, like almost all of those featured in the Smith and Spear collection, this process of shifting rightwards has been both necessary and successful. Ben Rosamond claims that, 'Labour emerged from the Policy Review process with a set of policies designed to meet the realities of industrial relations in the 1990s and carefully constructed to assuage both trade union and electoral opinion.'[13] Martin Smith concludes that, 'The importance of Thatcherism is that it has allowed Neil Kinnock the space to transform the party more successfully than any previous leader.'[14]

Indeed for some people the process has only just started and needs to be propelled forward at brusque speed. Pete Alcock celebrates Labour's 'advances in policy debate about welfare policy which have been made throughout the Thatcher years' and bemoans only that 'service delivery' still has not permeated the party's thinking.[15] With the Commission for Social Justice which has been set up by John Smith eagerly considering whether to target benefits and how to hold down wages, people like Alcock may soon have new triumphs to celebrate.

It is remarkable that these writers have such a bland acceptance of Labour's betrayal of its own supporters—and also fail to ask simple questions about whether the whole process has been a success. Have working class people benefited from the anti-union laws, privatisation and heavier defence expenditure—all parts of Labour's 'modernising'. Shouldn't the leadership be held responsible for Labour's failures and shouldn't they look squarely at the real results?

One of the sharpest consequences of Labour policy becoming more like the Tories' is a declining and demoralised Labour membership. 'One of the central lessons of the general election', said Labour's general secretary Larry Whitty after the party's defeat, 'is that Labour did best where it had an active campaign, and that is much easier with a large party membership.'[16] Academics Patrick Seyd and Paul Whiteley estimate that if Labour had 300,000 more members, it would have won 40 percent of the vote in 1992, not 34 percent. But Labour's membership is shrinking.

Seyd and Whiteley's book, compiled with the help of the Labour Party, provides a devastating insight into the collapse of Labour's membership and gives enough information to explain why it has happened. *Labour's Grass Roots, the Politics of Party Membership* is not a left wing analysis. It is an academic text which blames the left for many of Labour's problems. But it provides very valuable material which destroys the myths put forward by people like John Smith.

Labour's membership peaked in 1952 at over 1 million. From then on it declined. The method of counting members (each constituency had to register at least 1,000 between 1963 and 1980) hid the scale of the decay. But when a more honest system was adopted in 1981, the supposed membership of 666,000 was shown to be only 348,000. Today Labour claims around 260,000 members of which only 200,000 have paid the appropriate subscription.[17]

John Evans, the chair of Labour's finance working party, told the 1992 conference that almost half the present membership paid a reduced rate of £3 a year. As the cost of providing them with a membership card and *Labour Party News* was £3.50 a year, Labour was in the bizarre situation of losing more money the more it recruited.[18] The party survives financially because of the unions (who provide half the funds) and a core of 75,000 people who have a standing order to the party. Most central are the 28,000 people who give £5 a week. But this is no long term solution. Indeed, Evans told delegates, 'The general election defeat has left Labour with its most serious financial problems in its history. The party on the ground in many areas has deteriorated and its organisation weakened.'[19]

A confidential report to the national executive from the finance working party last December said that on present trends individual membership would fall to 200,000 and union affiliation fall by a further 1 million within four years unless remedial steps were taken.

Britain's largest union, the TGWU, has decided to slash affiliation from 1,070,000 last year to 750,000 in 1994. So despite an increase in affiliation fees from £1.60 to £1.80 per head, the TGWU will pay £320,000 a year less by 1995.[20] The union currently sponsors 38 MPs including such luminaries as Neil Kinnock, Margaret Beckett, Gordon Brown and Tony Blair. Their ranks will be thinned to 25. This will probably be done by 'natural wastage' although some branches have urged that Brown and Blair be ditched immediately for their support for breaking the link with the unions.

What no Labour leader can suggest is a way to staunch the haemorrhage of members. Yet this disintegration is not inevitable. It is certainly not, as some have suggested, because of changes in the pattern of industry. In 1955 there were 45 local parties with membership of more than 3,000. They were by no means all in areas which are now associated with strong Labour organisation. Constituencies with very high memberships included Woolwich West, Lewisham South, Faversham (in Kent), Eastleigh (in Hampshire) and Southampton Test—precisely the sort of places which are now frequently written off for Labour. There were thriving Labour clubs with big and active memberships in Swindon, Reading and Bristol.[21]

These branches recruited workers in traditional industries and also from the developing electronic, engineering and manufacturing sectors. A party with this many members had what Seyd and Whiteley call 'ambassadors to the community' everywhere. On each housing estate and in every factory there were Labour Party members. They were often fairly passive members, but they were crucial in arguing Labour's alternative to the people with whom they lived and worked. They challenged the 'common sense' right wing ideas peddled by the media.

A study of south London makes it clear that the local Labour Party was once an established part of the local community. From the 1930s onwards it was 'a centre of social and political life'. But by the late 1960s it had become nothing more than a 'rusty and seldom activated election machine.'[22]

Labour's membership has not only declined, its composition has also been transformed. 'The typical party member is a middle class man,' say Seyd and Whiteley.[23] There are very few young members—just 5 percent are under 26. A study by a team from Sheffield University showed that the average age of members was 48![24] This incredible statistic is easily explained and will stand as an example of how Labour cuts its own throat.

In 1983 there were 495 Labour Party Young Socialists branches and the national LPYS was very active.[25] But to the leadership's horror, the dominant voice was that of *Militant*. So as a part of making Labour electable, the youth section had to be purged. Unfortunately for Labour, in the process of saving the innocent youth section from the hands of 'unrepresentative extremists', the leadership also destroyed it. During the miners' strike the number of LPYS branches rose to an unprecedented 581. But none of this persuaded Tom Sawyer, the 52 year old chair of the NEC's youth committee, from issuing proposals for reform. Sawyer leaned heavily on work by ex-student activists John Mann and Phil Woolas who damned the LPYS as 'moribund' and 'insignificant'. Their recommended remedy was 'mass collective activity' for young people and 'political education'. Labour, they said, should aim its youth activities 'almost exclusively at teenagers' and stage 'large scale cultural and social activities'. The age limit should go down from 26 to 21, various local structures should be abandoned and more power should be held at the centre.[26]

When Sawyer's proposals were sent out for consultation 85 percent of replies were opposed. They were implemented regardless. Certainly the 'moribund' LPYS was transformed by Sawyer's plans. By 1990 the boring old 581 branches had been changed to 52. They had almost 300 members between them. Labour thus managed to organise 0.003 percent of youth in its target range. By the 1993 conference there were just 18 youth sections left. So, after a furious debate (about the organisation's name—one suggestion was 'Rosebuds'), Labour plans a fresh approach and a relaunch of its youth section as 'Young Labour'. To cover up the lack of numbers, Young Labour branches can cover several constituencies.

Nor is the party just older. Its class base has shifted. A party which was once composed largely of workers is now dominated by well intentioned members of the new middle class. They are committed to Labour ideas, but they are not in the main rooted in the workplaces and housing where most working class people, and most Labour voters, spend their time. Just one in four members are manual workers. Only 17 percent live in council houses compared with 25 percent of the whole population and 39 percent of Labour voters.[27] There are as many Labour members in the lecturers' union NATFHE (membership 70,000) as there are members in the public employees' NUPE section of the UNISON union (membership 580,000).[28]

Of course most teachers and lecturers are workers. But people at or near the top of these professions are not. And it is these people which Labour seems to be good at attracting. Less than half of Labour's members consider themselves to be working class. Some 49 percent of Labour's members (compared with 14 percent of Labour voters) are defined by Seyd and Whiteley as belonging to the 'salariat'—which is a higher occupational classification than routine non-manual.[29] Two thirds of Labour voters have a household annual income of *under* £10,000 whereas two thirds of Labour members have a household income of *over* £10,000. One in five Labour members has a household income of over £25,000.[30]

There are not enough Labour members and they are not in the right places to challenge consistently the media's version of events. Labour has launched repeated membership drives. Again and again the leadership have called for more people to be recruited but each time it has failed. In 1980 a party enquiry reported that 'an increasing membership must be of prime importance to the future work' and in 1987 Neil Kinnock headed a (completely ineffective) campaign to push Labour's membership back up to 1 million.

The want of influence which flows from a declining membership is reinforced by Labour's lack of a newspaper. In 1983 the party had two regular publications—*Labour Weekly* and *New Socialist*. Neither could by any stretch of the imagination have been described as lively or popular. But they did aim to carry Labour's policies to a wider audience. The Kinnock leadership closed down *Labour Weekly*, ostensibly because it was losing money, but *Labour Party News*—the members-only magazine which replaced it— was a far greater drain on resources. Between 1986 and 1990 it cost the party £750,000.[31]

Seyd and Whiteley now argue that Labour needs to be 'energized' at the grass roots level. But their book produces a wealth of material which can be used to demonstrate precisely why Labour has such a small and demoralised membership. Put bluntly, Labour's policies are unpopular with its own members. In almost every area where the leadership has insisted on a 'modernising' sharp move rightwards, a consistently large majority of the members are committed to 'old style' attitudes. Two thirds agree that 'the central question of British politics is the class struggle between labour and capital.' Yet Labour routinely expels people who resurrect the old bogey of 'class politics.'[32]

Over 70 percent of members are in favour of more nationalisation and an overwhelming 82 percent want the industries privatised by the Tories returned to public ownership. Yet at the last election Labour promised only to take a controlling stake in water and continue the sell-off of British Telecom. Labour pledged to keep nuclear weapons for as long as any other country had them, but 72 percent of members say Britain should have nothing to do with nuclear weapons.[33]

Perhaps most remarkably, 72 percent think workers should be prepared to strike in support of other workers, even if they do not work in the same place.[34] The idea of backing solidarity and sympathy strikes is absolute anathema to Labour's leaders. Left wingers who have been pushed to the very edge of the party turn out to be more popular than some members of the leadership. So, for example Dennis Skinner scored higher (in 1991) than Roy Hattersley.[35]

Given the disenchantment with many of the core policies presently pushed by Labour it is easy to explain one of the book's most important findings—that 43 percent of those interviewed are less active today than five years ago compared with just 20 percent who say they are more active.[36] A follow up study released this year showed that the gap between the percentage of members who felt themselves to be less active and those who felt themselves to be more active has grown from 23 percent in 1989-90 to 26 percent in 1992.[37] Only 56 percent of members had done any activity at all in 1992 (compared with 82 percent in 1990). Over 40 percent had not even put up a poster (in an election year) or sent money or attended a single meeting.

Of the most important reasons members gave for leaving the party, 25 percent mentioned Labour's abandonment of its basic principles. Also crucial was 'the move too far to the right'. A further 25 percent expressed dissatisfaction with specific policies of which the most important was Labour's support for the Gulf War. In addition to the move rightwards in policy, there are other important factors which explain why Labour members are now less active and do not try to recruit others to the party. One is the systematic witch hunt by the leadership against constituency activists.

Seyd and Whiteley found that the more left wing you are, the more likely you are to be an active Labour member. Yet the left have been hounded at every turn. Humiliated, disowned and threatened with expulsion they have become more passive—or torn up their card. Labour says it wants more members but it shuns their participation and rides roughshod over the decisions made by those members at conference. It calls for an election effort by members but it disdains public meetings and focuses the whole campaign on TV events and photo opportunities. In addition, almost a third of active Labour members are presently councillors. Their experience is of implementing unpopular Tory policies which directly harm the people who elected them. Some accept this as necessary, some indeed seem to revel in it. But many others are repelled and fade away.

Given all this evidence of the gap between the members and the party hierarchy, it might seem incredible that Labour's leaders ever got elected or manage to force their policies through conference. But the problem is that for all their anger at Labour's move right, the members are trapped by the central belief of the party—that there is no alternative to winning power in parliament. When members are asked directly if Labour should abandon its principles to win an election, over 60 percent disagree.[38] But a clear majority are also for the 'modernisation' strategy— trimming policies to get votes.[39]

Although they cheer Tony Benn's speeches and applaud Dennis Skinner's assaults on the Tories, they vote for Tony 'law and order' Blair to front the party. Labour's whole tradition is that of bending every effort to capture parliamentary office. However much members may talk about a different set of principles, in practice they are paralysed by the grim fear of electoral unpopularity and what the media will say about 'loony' Labour activists.

And the problem with all three books mentioned so far is that they remain firmly inside this parliamentary tradition. Heffernan and Marqusee are superbly vitriolic about Kinnock, they record in glorious detail the betrayals of those who now head the party. But not once do they really ask why this happens. Were they all just nasty people? Were they all simply consumed by a desire for power? Perhaps some of them were. But many started out as good left wingers before, in a process which has been repeated over and over again during the last century, becoming what they are today.

Neil Kinnock did vote 84 times against the cuts and closures of the Wilson-Callaghan government (a *Labour* government), he did defend the miners' mass picket of 1972—violence and all. What broke him and a thousand others was that concentration on office rather than the struggle. Heffernan and Marqusee can recognise that the miners' strike was the most significant event in the 1980s, but they still focus utterly on Labour as the place for socialists.

They may regard struggle as central, but they are completely wedded to a party which has, even in its best moments, relegated struggle to second place. This means Heffernan and Marqusee do not have a solution. All they can hope is that, despite the best efforts of the Labour leaders, struggle will revive. That would definitely force Labour leftwards. But as the journey from 1981 to 1992 showed, winning positions, policies and constitutional change inside the Labour Party is building on sand. What matters is developments outside the party. Even here there is no automatic link between a revival in confidence and a growth in

Labour membership. A Labour press official told me that the party had 'probably recruited about 1,800 people more than they expected between October 1992 to January 1993.' 'Of course that could be something to do with the computer and anyway it's less than the Trots,' she told me glumly before realising the source of the enquiry.

Yet for all its problems Labour is not finished. Unlike the fashionable columnists in the *Guardian*, we should not write off the chances of John Smith's Labour winning the next election. The hatred of the Tories can be too great even for Labour to dissipate. The government is plainly capable of making such huge errors that virtually nothing can save them or—like the American Republican Party in 1993—of embarking on a madcap right wing agenda that alienates swathes of middle class support as well as most workers. If the union leaders can be pressured to put up even the semblance of a fight, struggle could drive out the government and one effect would be to put Labour in office.

Labour's tailing of the Tories does nothing to mobilise votes. But despite firm commitment to right wing policies and a horror of supporting struggle, Labour type parties have won elections recently in Spain, Australia and Greece. These parties won despite the handicap of either being, or recently being, administrations which were implementing vicious anti-working class policies. Today many voters have no memory of the last British Labour government and the Tory myths about its incompetence tend to fade when compared with the present rabble.

Even the most apparently dead party can sometimes revive. In 1968 the French equivalent of the Labour Party won just 16.5 percent of the votes and the following year Gaston Deffere, its candidate in the presidential election polled just 5 percent. Twelve years later the new Socialist Party founded by François Mitterrand was swept to victory. It then, of course, presided over a decade of cuts and austerity measures which saw it return to 20 percent in this year's legislative elections.

The Portuguese Socialist Party was formed in exile just two years before the 1974 revolution by a handful of doctors and lawyers. But in the heady conditions of revolt (and with money from the ruling classes of Western Europe) it mushroomed ahead of its rivals in time to help stifle the Portuguese revolution and restore 'social peace'. Moreover Labour still derives strength from the very union link which its leaders want to weaken. Despite Smith's 1993 'reforms', the trade unions still elect half the national executive, have a third of the votes for leader and account for 70 percent of the conference voting strength. This means that, even if very weakly, working class struggle finds an echo inside Labour through its organic links with organised workers.

So Labour can win the next election, although the haemorrhage of membership and the distancing from the unions will make it more difficult. But even if Labour does win it won't be a party committed to workers' interests and it won't hesitate to turn on its own supporters once in government. Moreover there are more important considerations for revolutionaries than the prospects of Labour's electoral success. Whatever has happened at the polls, Labour remains the party which the overwhelming majority of advanced workers define as 'their' party. Reformist consciousness—the idea that the only way to change society is a little at a time through the mechanism of the existing state—remains strong.

It does not depend on Labour winning office or delivering reforms. As long as capitalism exists this reformist consciousness will exist. Even large scale struggle has the effect of strengthening reformist ideas as well as revolutionary ones. Reformist notions can (and must) be overcome only when workers feel their own power and are given an alternative political leadership which is well enough rooted in the class to provide a viable alternative. Building such an alternative means both analysing Labour's failures and putting forward a different model.

At least Heffernan and Marqusee are angry about Kinnock, at least they want the fightback. Two other books reviewed here have none of that flavour. Seyd and Whiteley's book is very useful about the reality of Labour's membership. But you should avoid the 'rational-actor models of activism' and so on which assume that people join parties for reasons based on how it will transform their personal life chances rather than any wider considerations. Smith and Spear's book has the occasional useful fact but is essentially a collection of rather tedious and shallow essays delivered at what must have been a less than exhilarating seminar series.

An apparently different approach comes from Gregory Elliott. The early part of his *Labourism and the English Genius* is superbly biting about Labour's failings. He assaults the 'modernisers' economic agenda as 'wallowing in the ideas of socialism's opponents'.[40] He satirises the fact that 'The traditional Labour cycle—moderation and failure in government, radicalisation out of office and so on and on—has been broken in opposition by a leadership whose novel solution to the problem of unkept promises was to make virtually none.'[41] He attacks Kinnock's failure to nail the Tories over, for example, the sinking of the *Belgrano* in the Falklands and over the Westland affairs when 'pushing at an open door he managed to slam it on himself'.[42]

Elliott's history of the party is interesting. He says there are three phases to Labour's past. Firstly there is the period from 1899 to 1940 of 'classical social democracy', then the transition to Keynesian social democracy up to 1975, then the era of social liberalism. Elliott shows that even in its best moments the party's record, when not iniquitous, was derisory. It was either backing the foulest imperialist slaughter or claiming to tackle the deepest social problems with the smallest measure of reform.

He is also scathing about attempts to reform Labour by working inside the party. He attacks those whose 'addiction to inner party struggle invariably led them to mistake composited triumphs inside "the movement" for tangible victories outside.'[43] I would raise some questions about Elliott's description of Labour's history, but at least he is trying to confront the structural problems behind Labour's decline. The trouble starts when he tries to put forward an alternative.

Here we find that the most important element is deemed to be constitutional change in order to liberate the state and the economy from the influence of archaic commercial and finance capital. With the House of Lords gone, proportional representation installed, regional parliaments flourishing and the monarchy on the scrapheap, it would be possible for manufacturing interests to burn more brightly. What starts as a biting and effective critique of Labour's shortcomings ends up as an apology for the sort of Lib-Lab nonsense peddled by the archest 'modernisers'.

Elliott even projects this schema back into history. He criticises Ramsay MacDonald for cutting unemployment benefit and wages in 1931 as a solution to capitalist crisis. But his main wrath seems to be directed at MacDonald's rejecting the 'obvious option for the minority Labour government of formal collaboration or an "informal understanding" at any rate with the Liberals. For although they had extended full support to Baldwin during the General Strike they had thereafter undergone a radicalisation.'[44]

None of the books reviewed here puts forward real hope precisely because they are, from different viewpoints, about Labour from a Labour perspective. There is today a new anger among ordinary people about the system. Building a movement around those feelings and the struggles that result from them means starting from an alternative to Labour's tradition. It will be one which puts socialist principles before chasing the opinion polls. That backs every struggle, whatever the headlines in the *Sun* or the *Express*.

There are several books which it is well worth reading to understand how such a movement can be built. Duncan Blackie's pamphlet *Socialism and the Labour Party: a dream betrayed*[45] is an excellent introduction to both Labour's history and why Labour fails. Ralph Miliband's *Parliamentary Socialism* marries together the theory about Labour with a good history up to the 1960s. It shows that there was no 'golden age' of the party and is very helpful for the background to Labour's present problems. He insists,

Of political parties claiming socialism to be their aim, the Labour Party has always been one of the most dogmatic—not about socialism but about the parliamentary system. Empirical and flexible about all else, its leaders have always made devotion to that system their fixed point of reference and the conditioning factor of their political behaviour.[46]

He adds that Labour plays an important role in the maintenance of capitalist society,

Social democracy for most of its existence has been primarily engaged in political brokerage between labour and the established order. This is a function which is of crucial importance to modern capitalism.[47]

If you want to know what a Labour government felt like from the inside, Tony Benn's *Diaries* show the manoeuvres, the cynicism and the betrayals. The volumes covering 1973-77 and 1977-80 are particularly helpful. You might find Paul Foot's book *The Politics of Harold Wilson* in your library and its study of one man and his Labour administrations throws a sharp light on the whole Labour project. David Coates has written a series of works (mostly out of print unfortunately) all of which have some useful material. The include *The Labour Party and the Struggle for Socialism*[48] and *Labour in Power?*[49] which is devastating about the last Labour government.

If you are interested in what happened to Labour parties at a local level, Barry Hindess (in better days) provides useful material in *The Decline of Working Class Politics*[50] which looks at Liverpool. S Goss's *Local Labour and Local Government*[51] is heavy going at times and certainly not a revolutionary text but it has a close examination of Labour in inner South London. But the best book to pick apart Labour's tradition remains Cliff and Gluckstein's *The Labour Party—a Marxist History.*[52] It explains Labour's roots and how its whole tradition is one of a partial break from ruling class ideology and yet an acceptance of its central element—that 'national interest' comes before class interest. Most workers still look to Labour at elections. But their support is grudging and with few illusions that John Smith in Number Ten will make a lot of difference. It is well worth reading Cliff and Gluckstein's book to understand how we replace Labour's rotten tradition with something better. The task is not to try and rescue Labour from its present decline but to build a fighting alternative.

Notes

1 R Heffernan and M Marqusee *Defeat from the Jaws of Victory* (Verso, 1992), p142.
2 Ibid, p25.
3 Ibid, p34.
4 Ibid, pp42-43.
5 Ibid, p93.
6 T Cliff and D Gluckstein *The Labour Party—a Marxist History* (Bookmarks, 1988), pp357-358
7 R Heffernan and M Marqusee, op cit, p95.
8 Ibid p97
9 M Smith and J Spear, *The Changing Labour Party* (Routledge ,1992), p17-18.

10   R Heffernan and M Marqusee, op cit, p322.
11   Ibid, p10.
12   Ibid, p302.
13   M Smith and J Spear, op cit, p100.
13   Ibid, p28.
15   Ibid, p150.
16   Larry Whitty's speech at the press launch of Seyd and Whiteley's book, June 1992.
17   P Seyd and P Whiteley, *Labour's Grass Roots* (Oxford, 1992), p16.
18   *Guardian*, 12 December 1992.
19   *Tribune*, 15 January 1993.
20   *Tribune*, 11 December 1992.
21   P Seyd and P Whiteley, op cit, p15
22   Ibid, p17.
23   Ibid, p28.
24   *Daily Mirror*, 17 December 1992.
25   R Heffernan and M Marqusee, op cit, p171.
26   Ibid, p71.
27   P Seyd and P Whiteley, op cit, p39.
28   Ibid, p35.
29   Ibid, p33.
30   Ibid, p39-40.
31   R Heffernan and M Marqusee, op cit, pp107-108.
32   P Seyd and P Whiteley, op cit, p125
33   Ibid, p125.
34   Ibid, p125.
35   Ibid, p153.
36   Ibid, p90.
37   *Guardian*, 25 September 1993.
38   P Seyd and P Whiteley, op cit, p134.
39   Ibid, p162.
40   G Elliott, *Labourism and the English Genius* (Verso, 1993), p20.
41   Ibid, p20.
42   Ibid, p138.
43   Ibid, p131.
44   Ibid, p42.
45   D Blackie, *Socialism and the Labour Party: a dream betrayed* (Bookmarks, 1991).
46   R Milliband, *Parliamentary Socialism* (Merlin, 1972), P13.
47   R Milliband, in *New Reasoner* No5, p46.
48   D Coates, *The Labour Party and the Struggle for Socialism* (Cambridge, 1975).
49   D Coates, *Labour in Power?* (Longmans, 1980).
50   B Hindess, *The Decline of Working Class Politics* (London, 1971).
51   S Goss, *Local Labour and Local Government* (Edinburgh, 1988).
52   T Cliff and D Gluckstein, *The Labour Party—a Marxist History* (Bookmarks, 1988).

The Socialist Workers Party is one of an international grouping of socialist organisations:

AUSTRALIA: International Socialists, GPO Box 1473N, Melbourne 3001

BELGIUM: Socialisme International, Rue Lovinfosse 60, 4030 Grivengée, Belgium

BRITAIN: Socialist Workers Party, PO Box 82, London E3

CANADA: International Socialists, PO Box 339, Station E, Toronto, Ontario M6H 4E3

CYPRUS: Ergatiki Demokratia, PO Box 7280, Nicosia

DENMARK: Internationale Socialister, Postboks 642, 2200 København N, Denmark

FRANCE: Socialisme International, BP 189, 75926 Paris Cedex 19

GERMANY: Sozialistische Arbeitergruppe, Wolfsgangstrasse 81, W-6000 Frankfurt 1

GREECE: Organosi Sosialisliki Epanastasi, c/o Workers Solidarity, PO Box 8161, Athens 100 10, Greece

HOLLAND: International Socialists, PO Box 9720, 3506 GR Utrecht

IRELAND: Socialist Workers Movement, PO Box 1648, Dublin 8

NEW ZEALAND:
International Socialist Organization, PO Box 6157, Dunedin, New Zealand

NORWAY: Internasjonale Socialisterr, Postboks 5370, Majorstua, 0304 Oslo 3

POLAND: Solidarność Socjalistyczna, PO Box 12, 01-900 Warszawa 118

SOUTH AFRICA:
International Socialists of South Africa, PO Box 18530, Hillbrow 2038, Johannesberg

UNITED STATES:
International Socialist Organisation, PO Box 16085, Chicago, Illinois 60616

The following issues of *International Socialism* (second series) are available price £2.50 (including postage) from IS Journal, PO Box 82, London E3 3LH.

International Socialism 2:60 Autumn 1993
Chris Bambery: Euro-fascism: the lessons of the past and present tasks ★ Chris Harman: Where is capitalism going? (part 2) ★ Mike Gonzalez: Chile and the struggle for workers' power ★ Phil Marshall: Bookwatch: Islamic activism in the Middle East ★

International Socialism 2:59 Summer 1993
Ann Rogers: Back to the workhouse ★ Kevin Corr and Andy Brown: The labour aristocracy and the roots of reformism ★ Brian Manning: God, Hill and Marx ★ Henry Maitles: Cutting the wire: a critical appraisal of Primo Levi ★ Hazel Croft: Bookwatch: women and work ★

International Socialism 2:58 Spring 1993
Chris Harman: Where is capitalism going? (part one) ★ Ruth Brown and Peter Morgan: Politics and the class struggle today: a roundtable discussion ★ Richard Greeman: The return of Comrade Tulayev: Victor Serge and the tragic vision of Stalinism ★ Norah Carlin: A new English revolution ★ John Charlton: Building a new world ★ Colin Barker: A reply to Dave McNally ★

International Socialism 2:57 Winter 1992
Lindsey German: Can there be a revolution in Britain? ★ Mike Haynes: Columbus, the Americas and the rise of capitalism ★ Mike Gonzalez: The myths of Columbus: a history ★ Paul Foot: Poetry and revolution ★ Alex Callinicos: Rhetoric which cannot conceal a bankrupt theory: a reply to Ernest Mandel ★ Charlie Kimber: Capitalism, cruelty and conquest ★ David McNulty: Comments on Colin Barker's review of Thompson's *Customs in Common* ★

International Socialism 2:56 Autumn 1992
Chris Harman: The Return of the National Question ★ Dave Treece: Why the Earth Summit failed ★ Mike Gonzalez: Can Castro survive? ★ Lee Humber and John Rees: The good old cause—an interview with Christopher Hill ★ Ernest Mandel: The Impasse of Schematic Dogmatism ★

International Socialism 2:55 Summer 1992
Alex Callinicos: Race and class ★ Lee Sustar: Racism and class struggle in the American Civil War era ★ Lindsey German and Peter Morgan: Prospects for socialists—an interview with Tony Cliff ★ Robert Service: Did Lenin lead to Stalin? ★ Samuel Farber: In defence of democratic revolutionary socialism ★ David Finkel: Defending 'October' or sectarian dogmatism? ★ Robin Blackburn: Reply to John Rees ★ John Rees: Dedicated followers of fashion ★ Colin Barker: In praise of custom ★ Sheila McGregor: Revolutionary witness ★

International Socialism 2:54 Spring 1992
Sharon Smith: Twilight of the American dream ★ Mike Haynes: Class and crisis—the transition in eastern Europe ★ Costas Kossis: A miracle without end? Japanese capitalism and the world economy ★ Alex Callinicos: Capitalism and the state system: A reply to Nigel Harris ★ Steven Rose: Do animals have rights? ★ John Charlton: Crime and class in the 18th century ★ John Rees: Revolution, reform and working class culture ★ Chris Harman: Blood simple ★

International Socialism 2:52 Autumn 1991
John Rees: In defence of October ★ Ian Taylor and Julie Waterson: The political crisis in Greece—an interview with Maria Styllou and Panos Garganas ★ Paul McGarr: Mozart, overture to revolution ★ Lee Humber: Class, class consciousness and the English Revolution ★ Derek Howl: The legacy of Hal Draper ★

International Socialism 2:51 Summer 1991
Chris Harman: The state and capitalism today ★ Alex Callinicos: The end of nationalism? ★ Sharon Smith: Feminists for a strong state? ★ Colin Sparks and Sue Cockerill: Goodbye to the Swedish miracle ★ Simon Phillips: The South African Communist Party and the South African working class ★ John Brown: Class conflict and the crisis of feudalism ★

International Socialism 2:49 Winter 1990
Chris Bambery: The decline of the Western Communist Parties ★ Ernest Mandel: A theory which has not withstood the test of time ★ Chris Harman: Criticism which does not withstand the test of logic ★ Derek Howl: The law of value In the USSR ★ Terry Eagleton: Shakespeare and the class struggle ★ Lionel Sims: Rape and pre-state societies ★ Sheila McGregor: A reply to Lionel Sims ★

International Socialism 2:29 Summer 1985
Special issue on the class struggle and the left in the aftermath of the miners' defeat ★ Tony Cliff: Patterns of mass strike ★ Chris Harman: 1984 and the shape of things to come ★ Alex Callinicos: The politics of *Marxism Today* ★

International Socialism 2:26 Spring 1985
Pete Green: Contradictions of the American boom ★ Colin Sparks: Labour and imperialism ★ Chris Bambery: Marx and Engels and the unions ★ Sue Cockerill: The municipal road to socialism ★ Norah Carlin: Is the family part of the superstructure? ★ Kieran Allen: James Connolly and the 1916 rebellion ★

International Socialism 2:25 Autumn 1984
John Newsinger: Jim Larkin, Syndicalism and the 1913 Dublin Lockout ★ Pete Binns: Revolution and state capitalism in the Third World ★ Colin Sparks: Towards a police state? ★ Dave Lyddon: Demystifying the downturn ★ John Molyneux: Do working class men benefit from women's oppression? ★

International Socialism 2:18 Winter 1983
Donny Gluckstein: Workers' councils in Western Europe ★ Jane Ure Smith: The early Communist press in Britain ★ John Newsinger: The Bolivian Revolution ★ Andy Durgan: Largo Caballero and Spanish socialism ★ M Barker and A Beezer: Scarman and the language of racism ★

International Socialism 2:14 Winter 1981
Chris Harman: The riots of 1981 ★ Dave Beecham: Class struggle under the Tories ★ Tony Cliff: Alexandra Kollontai ★ L James and A Paczuska: Socialism needs feminism ★ reply to Cliff on Zetkin ★ Feminists In the labour movement ★

International Socialism 2:13 Summer 1981
Chris Harman: The crisis last time ★ Tony Cliff: Clara Zetkin ★ Ian Birchall: Left Social Democracy In the French Popular Front ★ Pete Green: Alternative Economic Strategy ★ Tim Potter: The death of Eurocommunism ★

International Socialism 2:12 Spring 1981
Jonathan Neale: The Afghan tragedy ★ Lindsey German: Theories of patriarchy ★ Ray Challinor: McDouall and Physical Force Chartism ★ S Freeman & B Vandesteeg: Unproductive labour ★ Alex Callinicos: Wage labour and capitalism ★ Italian fascism ★ Marx's theory of history ★ Cabral ★

International Socialism 2:11 Winter 1980
Rip Bulkeley et al: CND In the 50s ★ Marx's theory of crisis and its critics ★ Andy Durgan: Revolutionary anarchism in Spain ★ Alex Callinicos: Politics or abstract thought ★ Fascism in Europe ★ Marilyn Monroe ★